KU-645-088

DOWN TO EARTH GOD

Michael Griffiths

HODDER AND STOUGHTON
LONDON SYDNEY AUCKLAND TORONTO

The poem on pages 84–5 is reproduced from *Psalms of My Life* by Joseph Bayly. Published by Tyndale House Publishers, Inc., © 1969. Used by permission.

The song on page 105 is by A. Snell and P. Thomson. Copyright © 1979 Thankyou Music. The full version can be heard on the album 'Something New Under the Sun'.

Unless otherwise indicated, Bible references are taken from the New International Version Bible.

British Library Cataloguing in Publication Data
Griffiths, Michael, *1928–*
    Down to earth God.——(Hodder Christian paperbacks)
    1. Christianity
    I. Title
    200   BR121.2

ISBN 0 340 35172 1

Hodder and Stoughton Editorial Office: 47 Bedford Square, London WC1B 3DP.

Down to Earth God

CONTENTS

FOREWORD

This book is intended for down to earth people who want a straightforward explanation of the Christian faith, in order to make up their minds about Jesus Christ. As an enthusiastic Christian, the author might wish to wax lyrical on such a subject, but will try to keep it cool, objective and matter of fact.

You may have been given this book to read by a friend who is already a Christian, or you may have got hold of it for yourself. It may be best to read a chapter at a time, and then think about that part before going on to the next. Each chapter is designed to cover a basic Christian doctrine. For your convenience, the main Biblical passages to be explained are printed in full in the text, but as the whole book inevitably derives its content from the Bible, you may prefer to check up on Bible references as you go along.

There may well be ideas you disagree with, but that does not matter, as the aim of the book is to set out the Christian faith as Jesus taught it and the apostles proclaimed it. After all, if you already agreed with it all, you would be a Christian already! If there are places where I have explained badly, or which are difficult to grasp, then talk it through with some Christian whom you know.

In its present form, the content reflects two series of talks given in the universities of Oxford and Durham in early 1979, though some of the material took shape earlier in giving similar series in the universities of Malaysia, Kuala Lumpur and Wellington, New Zealand. The later presentations included music, drama and poetry as well as preaching. I have tried to show something of these dimensions by including a little of the poetry and drama, and am grateful to Adrian Snell for permission to quote songs that he sang in Durham and Oxford.

Here are two vivid memories from the Oxford Mission to start you thinking and reading.

On the final night, Anne Atkins, a recent graduate studying drama, brought in a rather peculiarly shaped object. She told how a man found one in the forest and could not make out what it was meant to be used for. However he found the bowl-shaped end useful for drinking water from until it rotted away. He then planted it vertically in the ground and trained peas and beans up the strings until these also rotted away. Finally he used the remaining wooden part as fuel for cooking and keeping himself warm one cold night. As the last embers died away he was congratulating himself on his versatility. Walking next day in the forest, he encountered a girl carrying another of the strange objects, and said, laughing:

'I bet you can't find as many uses for that thing as I did!' The girl looked at him oddly for a moment, and then started to pluck a beautiful melody from the little African harp. The moral came over with enormous punch: it is possible to put one's life to all manner of useful and interesting purposes, and yet fail to discover what human life is really intended for. Anne finished by asking simply: 'When will you allow your Creator to play his music on you?'

On one of the earlier meetings held in the Oxford Union Debating Chamber, I noticed that the exit doors were marked Ayes and Noes so that students could register their response to debates as they went out into the lobby. On that night I finished by suggesting that while some of them might still be 'abstaining', that ultimately each one of us has to respond to Jesus Christ with acceptance or denial. The purpose of this book is to help you consider for yourself the claims of Jesus Christ and to decide intelligently for him or against him.

One of the drawbacks of evangelistic meetings is that people may be moved by the emotion of the moment to decide to become Christians without first weighing up carefully all that it involves. Speaking personally, I am always cautious lest I press people in a wrong way to follow the Lord Jesus, and if anything tend to lean over backwards rather than seem to be pushing them to make a decision there and then. By contrast the good thing about reading a book like this is that those human pressures are removed. You can read this book at your own pace, stopping to think or to check up on Biblical statements, and make up your mind in an unemotional way. Sometimes, even so, that decision may prove to be a soul-shaking and emotional experience – many big decisions are.

I was careful to say human pressures, because what you actually want to discover is whether God really exists or not, and will do some of his own persuading. You cannot leave God out of your thinking as C. S. Lewis tells in *Surprised by Joy*:

> Amiable agnostics will talk cheerfully about 'Man's search for God'. To me as I then was, they might as well have talked about the mouse's search for the cat. For I had always wanted above all things not to be 'interfered with'. I had wanted (mad wish) 'to call myself my own'. You must picture me alone in that room in Magdalene night after night, feeling whenever my mind lifted even for a second from my work, the steady unrelenting approach of him whom I so earnestly desired not to meet. That which I greatly feared had at last come upon me. In the Trinity term of 1929 I gave in and admitted that God was God, and knelt and prayed, perhaps that night, the most dejected and reluctant convert in all England.

But then if you too discover that God himself is doing the persuading, then that proves what you wanted to find out in the first place.

I hope that this book may help you to make the most wonderful discovery any human creature can make. In a down to earth way.

Michael Griffiths
Northwood, January 1985

Chapter 1

THE CREATOR WHO COMMUNICATES

> In the past God SPOKE to our forefathers through
> the prophets at many times and in various ways,
> but in these last days he has SPOKEN to us by his
> Son.
>
> (Heb. 1: 1–2)

One of the things I enjoy most in talking with another
person about God and trusting in Jesus Christ, is that spark
of communication between two people. You know perfectly
well as you start to talk that you do not agree with each
other: but there is that sense of respect for each other's
integrity and sincerity, and liking the other person for
themselves, whatever their views may be. There is no sense
in trying to score debating points: we want to share convictions and experiences, and if possible to arrive at some
conclusions.

I hope that something of that spark of communication
can exist even as you read what I have tried to express in
writing.

In a direct personal encounter, my concern as a committed Christian is to hear you, and to understand what if
anything you believe, and why. I have, in the Bible, the
example of encounters that Jesus himself had with various
individuals, and the real communication that took place
then. I must be careful therefore not to overstate my case,
exaggerate my experience, or spoil what I am trying to say
by putting the other person off by my pigheaded argumen-
tativeness, ungraciousness or just by not listening. If it does

not sound a little unfair, I should add that, as a Christian, I believe that God himself is also present when we discuss and will do his own persuading. The danger is that I myself will get in the way.

Because the Creator created communicating ('God SPOKE'), the spark when he comes into the discussion is all the greater. However as the other party may not believe that yet, perhaps that gives me an unfair advantage!

The good thing about writing a book, and trying to explain things to you by this means, is that my personality has less opportunity of getting in the way of your communicating with God. You are in control of the discussion, you can move at your own pace, and I am not there to argue back or to provoke you to teasing me with debating points that get us nowhere. But if the Bible is right, and there is a Creator who spoke to the Jews first through the prophets and then through Jesus, then as you read, the dynamics will be different because there is a God who is real, and present and communicating with you as you read and argue back. But why should that worry you? Is this not what you want to find out?

Perhaps I am going too fast already, and making assumptions you may not agree with. But then the Bible makes assumptions also. There is a God who has spoken.

THERE IS A GOD WHO HAS SPOKEN

The Bible makes no effort to prove this or to analyse its sources of information. It seems self-evident to the Bible that the Creator not only exists, but that he has also spoken – communicated. Provided you notice that this is an assumption, this does not matter because what we want to understand is the Bible's world-view, even when we do not necessarily agree with it.

Take this letter to Hebrew Christians quoted above. It begins by telling us that the Creator communicated in the past in a variety of different ways through the Hebrew prophets, and that he has spoken again through his son.

The whole Bible starts in the same way. Its very first words are:

> In the beginning God created the heavens and the earth . . . And God SAID: . . . (Genesis 1: 1, 3).

But we are not Hebrews, and God did not speak to our ancestors, and Jesus who claimed to be God's son lived two thousand years ago and we have no retrieval system to get him back, and no time-machine to go and look for ourselves, so how can WE know? How can we know that there really is a Creator out there who wants to communicate with us?

Because he has spoken.

When a voice comes out of the darkness, we know that there is somebody there, even if we cannot see them. We hear the voice, and respond at once: 'Who's there?' we want to know.

Seeing is not everything. An opposite situation can be imagined as even more frustrating, for it's impossible to get very far even with someone you can see, if they merely sit, withdrawn and silent, saying nothing. 'Why don't you say something?' we ask.

Take our communication now. I have been communicating with you for two or three pages. I don't suppose you have any doubts about my existence. Indeed you are well aware that if you wanted you could write to me, or arrange to come and talk. You may have never seen me, or heard the sound of my voice, but you have no doubts about my existence. Is it possible that the Bible might be a form of communication between the Creator and the creatures with whom he wants to get in touch, and establish relationship? Both Jews and Christians say that it is (though the former only think so about the first two-thirds of it).

After all human creatures long to communicate with each other. When I first went to Japan as a missionary the most horribly frustrating thing was not being able to communicate. You struggle to express yourself, but nobody understands. Japanese friends say something to you, but you cannot make out what it is they are saying. At times all you can do is smile and feel frustrated. Man is not only a rational being, but also a communicating being.

If man is indeed a created being, and not a mere organic fluke, then it seems somewhat improbable that beings who long to communicate should have been made by a Creator totally uninterested in communicating. The lesser must be the product of the greater. A mathematical computer must be designed by a mathematician. It is somewhat difficult to conceive of a talking human being created by a God who cannot or does not speak.

THERE IS A GOD WHO HAS CREATED

When the Book of Hebrews starts by saying that God has spoken, that gives us a way of knowing that God exists. Let me illustrate further.

I was travelling recently on British Airways which, like other airlines, provides a variety of entertainment in hour-long programmes over earphones. This distracts the passengers from thinking too much about what might happen if the engines should stop. Having enjoyed Sibelius's First Symphony, I turned to another channel and heard a certain Ronnie Corbett telling a funny story about a man cast away on a desert island, who after eighteen lonely years, is delighted when a beautiful girl wearing a wetsuit suddenly emerges from the sea. This rather inane story was just reaching a critical point when another voice interrupted: 'This is your captain speaking. We have now reached our cruising altitude of thirty-two thousand feet and our travelling time to Bombay will be five hours. Weather conditions are a little uncertain and we may experience some turbulence *en route*.'

The original programme then resumed, but maddeningly not at the point where it had stopped and Michael Flanders was now singing a little animal song. I was so peeved. There was nothing for it but to wait and listen to the whole programme right through all over again until reaching the same point, when, provided there was no further interruption, I could hear the end of the original story.

The parable is significant because the funny story was altogether trivial and insignificant, and had nothing at all to do with the real purpose of the journey. What the captain had to say about my destination was of crucial importance. Yet it seemed to be an irritating interruption as far as 'entertainment' was concerned. It is so possible for us to spend our lives absorbed with trivia and fail to ask the major questions about the meaning of our lives, and indeed, our ultimate destination.

Let's take this analogy a bit further.

Suppose you came back to me and said (being a bit perverse), 'But how on earth do you know that there really was a captain? Did you ever see him?' And I would have to reply: 'Well, no, I didn't actually see him, but I did hear him speak and he gave us some useful information about where we were going.'

You might on your part argue perfectly logically that I have no real evidence that the voice which purported to be the captain's was actually his, and no way of proving for certain that there was a captain on board at all. The whole thing might have been automated and it's impossible that anything could go wrong, go wrong, go wrong . . .

And for my part I would regard you as perverse, for is it reasonable to expect that a highly complicated piece of machinery like a Boeing 747 is going to take off all by itself and fly several thousand miles without somebody who knows what he's doing in charge of it all? And even if it was fully automated, surely somebody must have designed and built the thing in the first place.

What we have already discovered about the complexities

of human biochemistry, or of the whole of organic life, or
of mathematics or of the universe, reveals a complexity
which makes even a jumbo jet seem like a child's toy by
comparison.

Does it really make sense to argue that the 747 came into
existence all by itself owing to a fortuitous coming together
of molecules in suitable atmospheric conditions, and that the
whole machine took off entirely by itself, and isn't really
flying anywhere in particular? We could perhaps find remains
of other aircraft and put together an 'evolutionary series', and
argue that a Sopwith Camel lost its upper wing, evolved
into a De Havilland Mosquito, and then into a jumbo.
Could such a thing have happened by a random process? A
Creator and controller seem necessary for anything as com-
plex as our universe. But more than this. It also seems the
most acceptable hypothesis that rational, communicating
beings like ourselves should be the product of the creative
activity of a super-rational and super-personal Being, who
having put within us the desire to communicate, might
surely then be expected to communicate with us.

GOD SPOKE IN THE PAST
TO OUR FOREFATHERS

'At many times and in various ways' describes the Jews'
experience of the Creator communicating: his self-revelation
in the Law, the historical writings and the prophets. There
were the miracles, like the crossing of the Red Sea, for
example. Did they really happen or were they invented for
an earlier more credulous generation? Significantly accounts
of miracles are restricted to two great outbursts, the first
at the time of Moses, the exodus from Egypt and the occu-
pation of Palestine under Joshua; and the second in the days
of Elijah and Elisha, when Israel was in confrontation with
pagan religion. This is peculiar because if miracle stories
were merely later inventions to enhance the reputation

of popular heroic figures, it is difficult to know why no miracles are credited to the patriarchs Abraham, Isaac and Jacob or to their greatest kings like David and Solomon. Miracle stories are not larded haphazardly throughout the two thousand years of Old Testament history, but concentrated only in these two relatively brief periods.[1]

Is the Old Testament merely an account of Jewish ideas about God, or is it rather God progressively revealing more and more about himself to men? The writer to the Hebrews does not begin by saying 'Man guessed', but rather 'GOD SPOKE'. Agnostics have argued that even if God does exist, it is impossible for small, finite human beings to break out of a finite universe, to grasp the greatness of an infinite God. Christians agree entirely with agnostics and see the force of their objection. Human guesswork and speculation can only produce little gods made in man's own image. Subjective whimsies can only produce as many different gods as there are human beings. It is precisely for this reason that Christians reject a lot of what passes for 'religion' in this world as superstitious imagination.

It is certainly true that finite man cannot get out of his closed system. It is equally true that given an infinite Creator, he would have no problem breaking into our finite universe. Indeed this is what the Bible tells us: that the Creator has taken that initiative and broken through into our world in order to communicate with us. The Judaeo-Christian view therefore stands or falls on whether or not the Old and New Testaments are an authentic revelation, the Creator communicating with his creatures.

GOD HAS SPOKEN MORE RECENTLY TO US

The Hebrews passage goes on: '. . . in these last days [God] has spoken to us by his Son' (Heb. 1: 2).

Instead of the earlier revelation through a variety of

prophets at different times and in varied ways, this later revelation was given during one brief period through one person. The words of Hebrews balance a series of polished phrases with the one brief phrase 'by his Son' or more literally – for there is no possessive pronoun in the original – 'by Son'.

It is the same God who speaks, reminding us that Christian faith is not a mere two thousand years old, but goes all the way back to Abraham (1950 BC) and beyond. Christianity is as old as Judaism, and indeed continuous with it and a development from within it. So God is speaking in history, as well as unrolling and controlling it.

However, another objection naturally occurs at this point in our discussion. Is not a great deal of this alleged 'revelation' no more than myth and fairy tale? How do fairy tales start?

Once upon a time . . . are you sitting comfortably? 'Once upon a time, long, long ago there lived in a certain place, an old man and an old woman . . .' We are caught immediately by the excitement of a fairy story. I remember beginning some such explanation at Dozmary Pool on Bodmin Moor, where the arm clothed in white samite came out of the water and caught the sword Excalibur as King Arthur threw it in. 'How does she breathe down there? How could she see the sword coming? Won't it rust under water?' and so with a few well-chosen questions my computer-age child demolished the whole story. He would want to know exactly when, and where the old man and woman lived and what their names were . . . It doesn't matter, I reply impatiently, it's just a fairy story. It doesn't matter when and where and who they were.

The Biblical account is quite different. It may be less concerned with chronology than we are but it gives us the facts:

In those days Caesar Augustus issued a decree that a census should be taken of the entire Roman world.

(This was the first census that took place while
Quirinius was governor of Syria) (Luke 2: 1–2).

We are given long genealogies of the main characters, so
that we know exactly who they were (Matt. 1: 1–17; Luke 3:
23–38). We are given careful explanations of the start of
John the Baptiser's ministry:

> In the fifteenth year of the reign of Tiberius Caesar –
> when Pontius Pilate was governor of Judea, Herod
> tetrarch of Galilee, his brother Philip tetrarch of Iturea
> and Traconitis, and Lysanias tetrarch of Abilene –
> during the high priesthood of Annas and Caiaphas, the
> word of God came to John son of Zechariah in the
> desert (Luke 3: 1–2).

This detail is manifestly not the vagueness of myth and fairy
story, but a timemarker that can be matched with secular
history.[2]

THE QUALIFICATIONS OF THE SON

The expression 'by Son' surely needs some expansion and
explanation, and the writer to the Hebrew Christians does
this, and further describes the Son. It seems worth while to
examine what the Bible has to say about the dignity and
attributes of Jesus Christ of Nazareth.

> ... he, has spoken to us in his Son, whom he appointed
> heir of all things, and through whom he made the
> universe. The Son is the radiance of God's glory and
> the exact representation of his being, sustaining all
> things by his powerful word. After he had provided
> purification for sins, he sat down at the right hand of
> the Majesty in heaven (Heb. 1: 2–3).

God has spoken through him

Jesus not only spoke the truth but embodied it. The Gospel of John personalises the Word, who was in the beginning with God, and was God. He then says that the Word was made flesh or became a human being (John 1: 1,14). This is what theologians call incarnation, God revealing himself in a human person. Jesus himself claims again and again that he has come 'down from heaven' and 'into the world', been sent (John 3: 13; 6: 38; 9: 39; 18: 37; Luke 4: 43; John 3: 17; 6: 57; 7: 29; 11: 42). Can we believe his testimony about himself, and if he was deluded why did anyone believe what he claimed?

At any rate we should be clear that the Bible says that Jesus was not just a prophet who spoke the truth, but the embodiment of that truth, whose whole life and personality is an expression of God.

God has made him heir of all things

Many people have an unverbalised problem: what is the point of Christianity? What is the goal and purpose of what God is doing? The personal survival of individuals after death and posthumous benefits seem somehow a little petty, and perhaps based on unchristian motives, selfishness even.

The brief answer is that the expected 'Messiah' is to establish his kingdom, which is a wonderful new social order, the heavenly community. The author of Hebrews keeps returning to this theme. He writes of 'the world to come, about which we are speaking' (2: 5); 'they were longing for a better country, a heavenly one' (11: 16); and even 'here we do not have an enduring city, but we are looking for the city that is to come' (13: 14). The son is the heir of a permanent new society of which he is the inaugurator and the king. Does all this sound like a far-fetched fantasy? Almost space-fiction stuff?

Every new generation has its own dreams of Utopia. When in *The Making of a Counter Culture* Theodore Rozak was trying to describe what the New Left or the Hippies were looking for, he had to borrow expressions like 'the new Jerusalem' or 'the Holy City'. And he borrowed them from Christians, for throughout recent human history Jews and Christians have consistently provided the language to describe human aspirations for a perfect human society.

People today seem to have become disenchanted with the technocracy that offers programmed grins under plastic trees under the watchful eye of Big Brother. Often they have found satisfaction in fantasies about a perfect society: Middle Earth, Narnia and Watership Down in books; *Star Wars, Logan's Run, 2001* in film; and the craze for fantasy games is a part of this: if we can not make a real, perfect human society, then let us imagine one in a world of fantasy.

Human longing for the perfect society of which the Old Testament spoke, and for the heavenly Jerusalem of the New Testament, is to be fulfilled in Jesus, 'the heir of all things'. It is ironic that some modern people are rejecting historic Christianity because they regard it as myth, in favour of what they know to be pure fantasy.

This is partly the fault of Christian churches who, losing the Biblical dimension of community, have substituted a degenerated institution holding weekly ritual performances. The Church was founded by God as the beginning of the perfect new human community of which Jesus Christ is the heir. Becoming a Christian means a commitment to Christ's cause in building this new community.

God made the universe through him

Whether you agree with this or not, it is immediately obvious that the Christian view goes far beyond thinking of Jesus as merely a great prophet. The Book of Genesis in the Bible not only says that the Son was there when the universe was started, but that he started it! He was God's agent in creating everything. John (1: 3) and Paul (Colossians 1: 16) say exactly the same thing, if anything even more

powerfully. Before God could communicate with us, he first
created us through his Son. If this really is so, as Christians
believe, then I cannot disregard the person who brought me
into existence.

He shines with the brightness of God's glory

In the Old Testament period of revelation, God showed
himself in the tent of worship and the temple in Jerusalem,
as a brilliant radiance, sometimes called 'the Shekinah
glory'. It was so bright that Moses and the priests were
unable to enter. The apostle John wrote: 'The Word was
made flesh, and dwelt among us, (and we beheld his glory,
the glory of the only begotten of the Father,) full of grace
and truth' (John 1: 14 KJV). This was the shining light that
the three disciples saw in the face of Jesus on the mount of
transfiguration, and that the persecutor Saul of Tarsus saw
on the road to Damascus. John, in his vision of the risen
Christ, wrote that 'His face was like the sun shining in all its
brilliances' (Rev. 1: 16) and of the heavenly Jerusalem that
'The city does not need the sun or the moon, to shine on
it, for the glory of God gives it light, and the Lamb is its
lamp' (Rev. 21: 23). Poetic language perhaps, but perfectly
clear in what it is saying about Jesus. He is no mere super-
star, but the supreme outshining radiance of the glory of
God.

He is the exact likeness of God's own being

He is the exact expression of the divine nature and the very
image of the substance of God. The rare word used here for
'image' was used of the impression or stamp on coins and
seals. The Son is related to the Father as the image on a
coin coincides exactly with the impress on the die. Thus the
Revised Standard Version translates: 'the very stamp of his
nature'. Jesus is not a mere man, but as close to the being of
God as the impress of a seal is to the seal itself. Remember-
ing that the Jews abominated any kind of making of images,
as idolatry, it is indeed remarkable that this Jewish writer

writing to Hebrew Christians should say this about anybody. The greatest evidence for the deity of Jesus Christ is the way in which the first Christians wrote about him.

He sustains the universe with his powerful word

He is not only the one who made it all in the beginning, and the one who will inherit it all in the end, but the one who holds it in being now. Paul wrote similarly: 'In him all things hold together' (Col. 1: 17).

The old deist model saw the universe as a machine originally made by God, but now more or less running without him, following its own inexorable laws of nature. God is seen as like a human child who loses interest in his plastic model once he has completed it.[3]

By contrast the Bible insists that God is still intimately involved in sustaining the world he has made. The prophet Daniel says to King Belshazzar: 'You did not honour the God who holds in his hand your life and your ways' (Dan. 5: 23). The apostle Paul says to the Athenians: 'In him we live and move and have our being' (Acts 17: 28).

The Christian view also differs from pantheists who say that all particulars are part of God. God is everywhere present and active in maintaining all things in being. Therefore to ignore God is to disown the very maker and sustainer of our ungrateful lives. A great deal of discussion about God is superficial because our picture of him is not big enough, not terrible and awesome enough. This description of the Son says that my very breath is in his hands, and that he can withdraw it as swiftly as he gave it when I was born. Tom Howard in *Christ the Tiger* writes 'that he is in touch not with the pale Galilean, but with the towering and furious figure who will not be managed'.[4]

He made purification for sins

It is perhaps unfashionable to talk about sin in these tolerant days, but most of us have had our day spoiled, or spoiled the days of other people through malice, bitterness, jealousy and hatred. Try to suppress them as we will our consciences trouble us about such occasions.

However this phrase is significant in the context of the Book of Hebrews whose great theme is that Jesus can cleanse us effectively from the guilt and defilement of having sinned, in a way that Judaism is not able to do. The purpose of his coming into the world is to do something about human wickedness by dying on the cross. Repeatedly he tells his disciples about his coming death and afterwards reminds them that it was necessary for this to happen.

The greatness of Jesus is not only the majesty of who he is as the Son, but the magnitude of what he has achieved by his cross. Just as God's speaking through the Son parallels yet dwarfs the words of the prophets, so also the forgiveness made possible by the Son fulfils all that the Old Testament animal sacrifices by the priests only feebly portrayed. They are like candles dimmed by sunlight, or like the shadow which may precede a living person into the room. He is greater than all the prophets rolled into one, by virtue of his words, and greater than all the priests rolled into one by virtue of his works, namely that he made purification for sins. We shall say more about this in Chapters 3 and 4.

He sat down enthroned at God's right hand

This is picture language describing Christ's ascended glory in heaven. By contrast with Jewish priests who go on standing, offering sacrifices, and are never finished, the Son 'sat down' because he finished offering himself for men's sin once for all. On the cross he shouted, 'It is finished!' because he had completed all that needed to be done for men and women to be forgiven. No more sacrifices need to be offered. He finished both his words of revelation and his work of redemption. And so he is now 'seated' and 'enthroned'. It was also an essential part of the preaching of the first apostles that Jesus was now Lord, enthroned in heaven.

SO WHAT?

But what is the relevance of all this to me? you may well ask. Why is the writer to the Hebrews saying all this? The force of what he is saying is that if someone as great as this has spoken to us, how will we respond? He sums it up like this:

> We must pay more careful attention, therefore, to what we have heard, so that we do not drift away. For . . . how shall we escape if we ignore such a great salvation . . . which was first announced by the Lord?
>
> (Heb. 2: 1–3)

The writer envisages three main responses:

We may drift away from what we have heard

The word 'drift' can be used of a ring slipping off a finger, or a ship slipping her moorings unnoticed and drifting away from safety on to the rocks. Someone may have had a religious upbringing in a good Sunday school or church, and may have slipped away from it almost without noticing. 'What we have heard' is useless unless we act upon it for ourselves. However much our Christian parents may wish us to become Christians, they cannot do this on our behalf, because each of us has to make our own response to God – first-hand. We can not be second-hand Christians, but must each believe for ourselves.

In my first term as a student, I remember a visiting American evangelist, Dr Donald Grey Barnhouse, thundering out the words:

'You say you were born in a Christian home: If a cat has kittens in the oven, does that make them biscuits?'

God himself has spoken: first through the prophets and now finally by his Son.

What folly then to forget what he has said to us. Sometimes perhaps it may be a good thing for young people who have had a Christian upbringing to have this opportunity of examining the genuineness of their convictions. If they are not real, we shall certainly allow them to slip.

There is the possibility that we may neglect

The word 'ignore' or neglect can mean 'pay no attention' to the great deliverance offered to us through God's Son. When Jesus told the story of sending out messengers to invite guests to attend a great wedding banquet, and he explains how they ignored the first invitation, and yet other slaves are sent to invite them again, he used the same word as here: 'they paid no attention' (Matt. 22: 5). We may be people who never looked at the Christian faith seriously before, or perhaps our parents were either so hostile to religious ideas generally, or so neutral that it suggested to us that God was not very important anyway. No matter: you yourself have a personal invitation to the banquet. Will you disregard, neglect and take no notice of God's invitation?

The writer to the Hebrews is giving reasons for respond-ing to what God has spoken. The whole point of the long eightfold description we have examined is to make us realise how foolish it is to ignore a messenger with such credentials. Why would anyone in his senses wish to ignore such an invitation brought by such a winsome and convincing messenger? The word 'salvation' suffers from being a Christian jargon word, but it is used in the New Testament to speak of deliverance from prison, rescue from shipwreck or recovery from illness. We are offered a relationship with our Creator, reconciliation with God and fulfilment of the destiny for which we were created as human beings. To refuse such a message is to deny the whole purpose of our existence.

The writer says that he himself was not an eye witness to the events of Jesus's life on earth, but like us present-day Christians, believed as a result of the testimony of those who knew him, the apostles. They HEARD his words, and wrote them down so that we can READ them. They confirmed his words in their own experience, and found them reliable and dependable. God gave added confirmation we are told, through 'signs and wonders' and by 'various miracles'. This third miraculous period, recorded in the New Testament, was not a mere sensational outbreak of spiritual fireworks but an authentification of the credibility of the Son and of his apostles. The prophets through whom God spoke had said that when the Messiah comes:

> Then will the eyes of the blind be opened and the ears of the deaf unstopped. Then will the lame leap like a deer, and the tongue of the dumb shout for joy (Isa. 35: 5–6).

The third outburst of miracles then was seen as the necessary credentials of the genuineness of Jesus as the Christ Messiah.

We may pay much closer attention

If anybody speaks to us good manners require us to reply. If some great human being speaks to us we feel privileged to be noticed at all. If our Creator has spoken to us through his Son, as well as through the prophets, have we listened, heard and obeyed? Have we drifted away from what we heard in our youth? Or have we never so far paid any attention?

If Jesus is who this letter to the Hebrews says he is, and if our Creator is trying to communicate with us, then if we do not respond we are missing the whole purpose of our existence.

God has spoken. So we must answer. It would be stupid to maintain a stubborn silence pretending that we have not heard.

If we have doubts they must not be ignored, but must be carefully considered. Are we prepared to study the written records of what was spoken, to examine what purports to be our Creator's communication with us? Have you ever in your life examined the New Testament – as a thinking adult? Are you merely rejecting a childish, Sunday school understanding of Christianity? We may have been uncritical when we were younger, but that is no reason for avoiding a thoughtful, critical examination now that we are able to make it.

I have hardly ever met anybody who seriously and honestly considered the Christian faith as an adult who did not then become a Christian. It sounds arrogant to say this, but unbelievers are usually uninformed. I hasten to add that this ignorance has no direct correlation with intellect. You can be a brilliant philosopher but ignorant of what makes motorcars work. You may be a brilliant scientist and a complete Philistine where literature and art are concerned. 'Unbelievers' are people who are ignorant of the Christian faith. Those who are willing to examine the evidence of the Biblical documents and so cease to be ignorant, usually cease to be unbelievers. It is because some people deliberately choose to remain ignorant, that they remain unbelieving: but this is then wilful and culpable ignorance. If we have never studied the New Testament documents for ourselves as adults, then we cannot in honesty continue to regard the Christian faith as inadequate. It is not the Christian faith which is then in doubt, but our own intellectual integrity. It is just not honest to reject the Christian faith if we have never examined it.

A CHALLENGE

In a friendly way then, I would like to dare you to expose yourself to the evidence. You may not want to risk examining the Christian faith because of what you believe might be the consequences of doing so. But that would only prove that you are cowardly, not that the Christian faith is false! What matters is our integrity and an honest and fresh examination of the New Testament documents in order to

determine their truth or otherwise. It is possible to read one
of the gospels right through at a sitting, and I would invite
you to do that at least once in order to see afresh what sort
of person Jesus is.

I once asked a Canadian friend how he became a Christian.
He explained that he and his wife had come over to London
for the Coronation of Queen Elizabeth. As they stood outside Westminster Abbey in the pouring rain, they heard the
voice of the Moderator of the Church of Scotland say to the
Queen: 'This is the most valuable thing which the world
affords. This is the Royal Law. These are the living oracles
of God.'

These last words so struck him: could they indeed be the
living oracles of God, and has he so spoken to men? Yes,
that is what they are: the living oracles of God. So the next
day, when the shops opened, my friend went out, bought a
Bible and read it and shortly after believed.

The arms of the University of Oxford consist of an open
Bible with the words in Latin: *Dominus illuminatio mea*. It is a
prayer over an open Bible that the Son who is the radiance
of the glory of God will illumine me and fill me with light as
I read. May I suggest then at the end of this chapter, not
only that you start reading the New Testament, but that as
you open it you pray to the God who has spoken that he will
illumine you as you read.

Chapter 2

THE DOWN TO EARTH GOD

In a two-dimensional flat land, any visitor from an outside three-dimensional universe would still appear only as a two-dimensional figure. Thus, a cube would only appear as a square and might have difficulty in persuading sceptical flat-landers that there was a third dimension at all. A spherical body would only appear as a circle and though he might be able to vary his diameter, there would still be the problem of convincing the flat-landers that he had come 'from outside'.

When the Creator chose to appear in our world, he came as a man. We sometimes conveniently distinguish between the natural and the supernatural, but we have to appreciate the fact that, from God's point of view, the supernatural does not exist: it is all the one reality which he knows and has brought into being. We men regard everything which lies outside space and time as supernatural and so we are confronted with this man Jesus who made very remarkable claims.

Christmas underlines all that must have been involved for God to come 'down to earth'. What could it have meant for the Son of God to be born as a human, laid in a manger in the straw amidst the smells of the dung and urine of the cattle, and to embark upon the precariousness of human existence, being carried around as a weak and helpless human baby, totally dependent upon his parents and their attention to his bodily needs?

We might get some glimmering of an idea if we tried to imagine all that would be involved for us, as human beings, in getting 'down to earth' as an earthworm and spending all our lives wriggling around in a small patch of soil, conscious of vibrations but without a brain capable of appreciating all that we have been able to appreciate as human beings.

This, then, is what Christians believe about what is called technically the Incarnation, that is to say, God becoming flesh and coming down to earth to live among us. An early Christian hymn expresses it:

> Who, being in very nature God,
> did not consider equality with God
> something to be grasped,
> but made himself nothing,
> taking the very nature of a servant,
> being made in human likeness.
> And being found in appearance as a
> man,
> he humbled himself
> and became obedient to death –
> even death on a cross!
> Therefore God exalted him, to the
> highest place
> and gave him the name that is
> above every name,
> that at the name of Jesus every knee
> should bow,
> in heaven and on earth and under
> the earth,
> and every tongue confess that Jesus
> Christ is Lord,
> to the glory of God the Father.
> (Phil. 2: 6–11)

I want now to look more closely at some of the expressions used in this hymn about Jesus, especially in understanding why it is that Christians believe that Jesus is God come down to earth.

Being in very nature God

A modern translation has the opening phrase: 'He always had the very nature of God.' Saying that Christ from the beginning had the form of God means that in his own inner person he possessed the full reality of deity. He always had done. Jesus is truly and fully God and always has been. He did not come into existence for the first time at Bethlehem. This is a statement about the 'pre-existent' Christ. He claimed to have come from heaven and to have been sent to earth by his Father. Either this was truth or delusion. He declared himself to be unique, 'You do not know where you come from or where you are going: I know both.' We can begin to see that these claims of Jesus are crucial to our understanding of his personality. If indeed he was wrong about himself, then he may well have been wrong about most other things; and if he was wrong about himself, what he said about other things scarcely matters.

He did not consider equality with God something to be grasped

The pre-incarnate Christ refused to use his position as the unique image of God to exploit his privilege to seek honour and glory. He already held, as a personal possession, the dignity of a place in the Godhead. However, he was ready to wait until that time when the Father chose to proclaim him as 'Lord'. This could only happen when, in obedience to the Father's will, he became a man in order to save mankind. Instead of seeking to grab the glory, he deliberately stepped down in three great downward steps, only then to be exalted by God.

But made himself nothing, taking the very nature of a servant

What does this 'made himself nothing' mean? Does it mean that, in order to become a man, he first had to empty himself of deity? It does not say so, and indeed the previous clause, 'being in very nature God', implies the reverse. He did not leave his deity behind when he was taking the form of a servant.

Think of the everyday action of emptying a milk bottle into a jug. You can empty the bottle or empty the milk. What possessed full 'lactic reality' in a bottle continues to possess full 'lactic reality' in a jug. He brought his deity intact into the new circumstances. There is nothing here about abandoning divine characteristics, but only about assuming human qualities.

Made in human likeness

'Taking the very nature of a servant' means that he assumed human nature; 'in human likeness' means that he shared the reality of human appearance and was indistinguishable from any other male human.

And being found in appearance as a man

He entered totally into the reality of all that it means to live as a human being. So, having first asserted his divine nature, the hymn says that, while remaining truly God, he became truly man: assuming human nature, human appearance and human experience. His true stature was partly concealed by his mortality and his glory considerably veiled by his humility, but there is no suggestion that he gave up his divine pre-existence when he took on human existence.

He humbled himself and became obedient to death

In parallel with the phrase 'made himself nothing', the phrase 'humbled himself' points to a second, deliberate downward step. He first poured out his deity into human experience and he now pours out his mortality into death. Death, for Jesus, was an act of obedience. He deliberately emptied himself in becoming a human being, and humbled

himself to take the form of a servant, dressing himself with a
towel in order to wash his disciples' feet.

'Became obedient to death' provides the third great
theological statement so far. The hymn declares of
Christ: he is truly God, he became truly man and he truly
died.

Even death on a cross

These words spoil the metre, and are thought, therefore,
to be Paul's own added parenthesis to the words of the
hymn. It is not only that he died, but that he died such a
death. Execution by crucifixion would have been repulsive
to Roman citizens in Philippi, who enjoyed the privilege
of death by beheading! All men had for the cross that
revulsion which is normal for the instruments of execution.
I remember once standing at the crossroads at Caxton
Gibbet, where a gallows still stands and where, in this bleak
and desolate spot, a length of rope continued to hang from
the gallows, creaking in the wind. One naturally shudders
at the prospect of such a death.

But what was a matter of revulsion to Romans was an
even greater abomination to the Jews. The Law (Deut.
21: 23) said that he who hung on a tree was accursed of God
and, in Jewish eyes, the victim of hanging or crucifixion was
seen under ban of excommunication from God's Covenant,
and under sentence of God's wrath. It was not only that
the man who died on a cross suffered ignominy before men,
but also that, in the eyes of Jews, he was accursed and
disowned by God and in a particularly terrible sense, God-
forsaken.

The Jewish leaders were embarrassed because the theo-
logically ignorant common people were enthusiastically
espousing the impossible notion (it seemed to them) that
Jesus of Nazareth was the Messiah foretold by the prophets.
For this reason they must at all costs discredit him and
somehow find a way of destroying his 'face'. There is a very
colourful phrase in Japanese 'to rub mud in somebody's

face', meaning to deliberately discredit someone publicly and destroy their credibility.[1]

The Jewish leaders were asking how they could disgrace and discredit Jesus so that nobody could ever believe in him again. Somebody may have suggested stoning him for blasphemy. But the prophets had been stoned and were now honoured by the people. Then somebody had a brilliant idea: Let's get the Romans to crucify him. Then, so far from his being the Son of God, everybody would see him as being the accursed of God. That would destroy his credibility. He had talked about the glory which he shared with his Father; there was no glory in being executed on a Roman cross. He spoke of that power which the Father had given to him; let him cough out his life in weakness on the cross.

At first sight, it seems remarkable that the Jewish equivalents of the archbishops of Canterbury and York and a gathering of religious leaders should deliberately go to an execution in order to jeer at a dying man, 'Come down from the cross, if you are the Son of God! . . . For he said, "I am the Son of God"' (Matt. 27: 40–43). They were making certain that everybody got the point and that Jesus was thoroughly disgraced and discredited in the public mind. It was the greatest loss of face in history: 'His appearance was so disfigured beyond that of any man' (Isa. 52: 14).

The first section of the hymn has Jesus as its subject and speaks of his deliberate identification of himself with men. But the second half has God as its subject and tells of how he arranged a coronation for Jesus. First, there is elevation to the throne ('God exalted him'), then there is the proclamation of his new Name ('gave him the name that is above every name'), then offering him homage ('every knee should bow') and, finally, pledging allegiance ('every tongue confess').

Therefore God exalted him

Because of what Jesus has done in emptying and humbling himself and pouring out himself to death, God now exalts him. There is a clear reference here to Isaiah's prophecy, 'My servant . . . will be raised and lifted up and highly exalted' (Isa. 52: 13). The Creed declares, 'The third day he rose again from the dead, he ascended into heaven.' Here, however, the resurrection is passed over (we shall deal with it in the fourth chapter) as part of the ascension and the 'exalting' act of God.

Perhaps this is a good point to deal with two common difficulties. You may feel this idea of Christ coming down and being lifted up is merely reflection of an ancient and outdated cosmology of a three-storey universe.

Up and down, of course, are figures of speech rather than being strictly spatial. After all, even when playing snakes and ladders, we go up and down. We speak of being humbled to the dust and exalted to the skies. Our children tell us that they expect to go up next year, undergraduates are sent down, men are promoted upstairs, or elevated to the peerage. This does not commit us to believing in six-storey schools, universities on hills or a two-storey House of Parliament. These are perfectly understandable concepts.

Secondly, some people have problems in believing in the bodily resurrection of Jesus and that he rose from the dead, body, bones, flesh, blood and all. Surely, we are not meaning to say that there is a flesh-and-blood man in heaven? Is it not enough just to say that the Spirit of the eternal Jesus goes marching on?

However, this 'John Brown's body' explanation of Christianity just will not do. We know that John Brown's body lies mouldering in the grave while his soul goes marching on, and the idea of liberating the slaves continued, but does this do justice to what Christians believe about the resurrection of Jesus?

Some have said that this is just picture language and that the resurrection and the ascension are seen as a vivid and existential way of explaining the great value which the Christian Church has set upon Jesus. However, if we think of the ways in which the Jewish leaders deliberately humiliated Jesus we can see that only a real resurrection would be sufficient to vindicate him and restore his credibility. He did not die in triumph, but in shame and disgrace. If there is no real resurrection, then there is no triumph and no possibility of singing 'Glory, glory, hallelujah'. For why should the soul of a condemned criminal go marching on anywhere, and why should anyone follow him even if it did?

This particular passage makes it abundantly clear that the resurrection-ascension is not picture language expressive of the mind of the Church, but rather true events expressive of the mind of God. Just as the Jewish leaders looked for a way to show everybody that Jesus was disgraced, so God found an even more vivid way of showing that he vindicated his son by raising him from the dead and highly exalting him. As Alec Motyer expresses it, God said 'I will show there is none like him: I will raise him from the dead. I will show there is none above him: and set him at my right hand.' The only thing that can wipe away such a horrible and distressing disgrace is to demonstrate plainly his grace by showing that Jesus really is who he claimed to be. And only a real resurrection would reinstate him after such a disgrace. How could anyone ever believe in him again unless he had been raised up by God himself? It is done deliberately in unhurried fashion: after three days he is raised and after forty days he is exalted.

Now he is crowned and elevated to the throne, the cosmic King sovereign over the universe. Now he is elevated to the position which he refused to take previously. He who quite deliberately stooped to the humiliation of death is deliberately elevated to equality with the Father, and is now openly seen to merit the homage and allegiance of men.

And gave him the name that is above every name

The name which he would not seize and refused to take for himself he is now given.[2] It cannot be the name Jesus which is the name above all other names but, as is clear from the end of the hymn, the name Lord (*Kurios*). In the Greek version of the Old Testament, the Septuagint, this Greek word is used to replace the personal Name of God (Yahweh).

It is not, therefore, that deity was conferred upon Jesus, for he was already in the form of God from the beginning, but rather that he had bestowed upon him what was unmistakably God's own personal name.

This was necessary because many might otherwise assume that in the process of becoming fully man, he was no longer fully God. This is indeed a difficulty that some have expressed.

By proclaiming that Jesus is henceforth to be called Lord, God the Father has exalted him in a deliberate and considered act, and given him his own name in token of his co-regency, sharing not only the throne of the Father but his very name.[3]

There is a wonderfully vivid and colourful description of the great throng of created beings pledging their homage to Jesus as he is crowned as King and Lord:

And every tongue confess that Jesus Christ is Lord, to the glory of God the Father

The final word of the hymn is Father, so that far from the Son being seen as a rival to his Father, this public recognition and confession of his Lordship is to the glory of God the Father. There will be those who bow the knee and whose tongues are loosed to confess Jesus as the Lord they have long served and loved. There are others who have rejected and disregarded his claims, who will find that his overwhelming majesty will bring them to their unwilling knees, admitting a long unacknowledged truth too late.

This passage carries, then, its own challenge: are you prepared to acknowledge him as Lord and pledge your loyalty to him? Are you willing to give him your allegiance now?

As citizens of Rome, the Philippians would know that the titles Saviour and Lord were both used as special titles in worship of the emperor who might come to visit them from Rome. It was the Philippians' boast that they were citizens of Rome, living in a Roman colony. Later on in his letter to them, Paul applies this picture to the Philippians, deliberately picking up some of the Greek words from the hymn we have looked at:

> But our citizenship is in heaven. And we eagerly await a Saviour from there, the Lord Jesus Christ, who by the power that enables him to bring everything under his control, will transform our lowly bodies so that they will be like his glorious body (Phil. 3: 20–21).

The Philippian Christians, he says, are a colony of heaven. Their citizenship is in heaven and they are looking for a royal visit, not of a Roman emperor, but of the King of kings, the Lord Jesus Christ. In Chapter 2 he has spoken of Christ's coronation and in Chapter 3 he speaks of his second royal coming in triumphal glory.

These words suggest the reason why Jesus emptied and humbled himself. He took our form in order to give us his. He came to earth, in order to take us to heaven. The New Testament says that he became the first fruits of a new humanity. In more modern language, we might say that he became the prototype of a new 'Jesus people' or, in the language of science fiction, that a new clone has been established. Paul explains that the purpose of the gospel is that we might be 'conformed to the likeness of his Son, that he might be the firstborn among many brothers' (Rom. 8: 29). C. S. Lewis expressed it so graphically in saying that the purpose of the Christian message is that we might all become 'little Christs'.

Response to Jesus, in giving him our allegiance as Lord, carries with it the anticipation of being transformed by him into new men and women. Becoming a Christian is not merely accepting a new set of beliefs, but becoming a new person through the supernatural work of God in our lives.

Chapter 3

THE LOVER OF THE UNLOVABLE

So Christ came down to earth and became man in order to die on the cross. But the question naturally arises, why did he do that and why was that necessary? The New Testament spells it out very plainly.

> At just the right time, when we were still *powerless*, Christ died for the *ungodly*. Very rarely will anyone die for a righteous man, though for a good man someone might possibly dare to die. But God demonstrates his own love for us in this. While we were still *sinners*, Christ died for us. Since we have now been justified by his blood, how much more shall we be saved from God's wrath through him! For if, when we were God's *enemies* we were reconciled to him through the death of his Son, how much more, having been reconciled, shall we be saved through his life! (Rom. 5: 6–10, my italics).

'God demonstrates his own love for us'. The love of God is a cliché which we perhaps take for granted because, after all, it's God's business to love isn't it? And because we love ourselves most of the time, it does not surprise us that God should love us. It is so unremarkable that, to many it now seems rather irrelevant. It leaves us cold.

Talking of God loving us may smack a little of sentimental Victorian Christianity: what J. B. Phillips called 'heavenly bosom-ism', that is the language of 'safe in the arms of Jesus' or 'let me to thy bosom fly'. God is not

sloppy or sentimental, but vigorous and realistic in his love
for us.

These verses say that God has demonstrated or proved
his love towards us. However if we have never so far responded to God's love, then it is not yet proven as far as we
are concerned. We are not yet convinced that God loves us.
These verses should help to convince us.

A major problem for many young people is – whom to
love and how to show it! This passage tells us whom God
loves and how he has shown it.

WHOM DOES GOD LOVE?

You and I like some people more than others and dislike
some people more than others. The people we like are
usually likable people, pleasant and attractive, and as we
like them, they like us – a modest, mutual admiration
society. Britain is full of such pleasant, likable people –
decent, clean-cut, British people. The irony is clear!

We have a stronger feeling we call *love* towards a smaller
circle. We love our parents first because they love us, and
we feel very secure and accepted. Often, we accept the
love of parents and brothers and sisters as a right when
we are small and only later begin to appreciate them and
return their love; with sweethearts and spice (or whatever
the plural of spouse is), we love them because they return
our love. Here, we are most particular; we have high standards of expectation for character, appearance and vital
statistics. We have our perfect dream girl or her mascu-
line equivalent. She must be the most beautiful, shapely,
intelligent, sweet-natured girl in the world. He must be
the most intelligent, athletic, dashing, dishy, strong,
well-mannered, sensitive man you can find. And, if we
should be so fortunate as to happen to find such a paragon,
we can only hope that they will not be quite so fussy
about us.

I remember arranging a marriage for a Japanese Christian who, having been ill with tuberculosis for many years, was in his mid-thirties before he was finally cleared to take a job and marry. We were invited to help to look for a suitable bride for him and, in due course, we arrived at that highly emotional moment when these two met each other for the first time. You can imagine the two of them standing there and looking each other up and down. My friend was not a paragon of the kind described above and, partly because of his ill health, perhaps not the most prepossessing and dashing of men. However, he was quite pleased at the girl we had found for him, and came out with the memorable remark: 'If you don't think much of me, it must be because I prayed harder than you did!'

I think the point is made, however, that love is, generally speaking, a response to worthiness and winsomeness in somebody else. We love people who are lovely, or lovable, or who love us in return.

'God demonstrates his love for us' because his love is so different. The people whom he loves are not in his eyes particularly lovely or lovable and, often, they do not love him at all. He is not taken in by our outward appearance, our smooth exterior, our expert make-up, our good manners or our snazzy clothes. Even when we are dressed up to look our best, he knows all the secret motives and desires of our hearts.

What kind of people, then, does God love? The Bible verses we quoted give us some clues.

Sinners

God loved us 'while we were still sinners'.

Because there is some confusion in people's minds about what Christians mean by sin, it is important to try to clarify a number of different basic meanings.

Firstly, *intentional sins*. These are premeditated and deliberate acts which our consciences tell us are wrong, selfish and displeasing to God. It means things we do wilfully, deliberately and persistently, even though we believe them to be wrong. Such sin is open defiance of God and the Ten Commandments. Why should I obey God? Why shouldn't I do things which God forbids? It's what Piggy in Golding's *Lord of the Flies* calls 'against the rules, laws and rescue'. Such deliberate transgression breathes defiance of God's commandments as good and intended for our well-being. On this understanding, then, sin means deliberate and premeditated evil-doing. It's when we *plan* to steal, or hurt, or to be faithless to a partner.

Secondly, *impulsive sins*. These are things which we never meant or planned to do. When we lose our tempers, it's not because we planned or plotted to do so, but because we suddenly found we could not contain ourselves. We may say mean and malicious things to hurt other people, or suddenly we are tempted to lie or lust or cheat or shoplift.

The commonest word used for sin in the Bible means failing to hit a target. We aim at something good, but we keep missing it. Impulsive sins are those in which we say, 'I was carried away, my tongue ran away with me, I could have bitten it off, I don't know what came over me.' And, because we never planned to do these things, when we have done them we feel sorry about them. We feel guilty about deliberate sins beforehand, because we are planning to do something we believe to be wrong and our conscience is troubling us. With impulsive sins, there is no premeditated intention to sin, and one feels distressed and fed up with oneself afterwards.

Thirdly, *indwelling sin*. This is something much more fundamental; this is the root from which the fruit of intentional and impulsive sins springs. It is a bias of the personality, a distortion of our being, arising from hidden malice, resentment, envy, selfishness and bitterness in our hearts. This meaning of 'sin' is not so much describing crimes we commit as an underlying disposition of character.

Golding's book *Lord of the Flies* is the story of what happens when a group of very decent British schoolboys are marooned on an island paradise and how they spoil it all. If you like, it is an example of the existence of original sin. The book closes with its hero 'Ralph, with filthy body, matted hair and unwiped nose weeping for the end of innocence, the darkness of man's heart . . .' It is this darkness of man's heart which the Bible would call indwelling sin.

There is a story from Japan which helps to illustrate this. There were two very beautiful Japanese girls who lived in Aomori Prefecture, at the most northerly tip of the island of Honshu, who were very close friends. One day, the two of them saw an advertisement for a beauty contest and giggling behind their hands, the two of them decided it would be fun to go in for it.

In due course, these two beautiful girls, dressed in their most expensive kimonos, entered the competition and one of them was chosen to be Miss Aomori, the most beautiful girl in Aomori Prefecture, while her friend, unfortunately, came much further down the list. And then a strange thing happened. Although, up to this point, they had been very close friends, their relationship became increasingly cool. The heart of one girl was filled with pride; was she not the most beautiful girl in Aomori Prefecture! The heart of the other girl was filled with envy and jealousy and, in the end, this jealousy so consumed her, that she threw a bottle of acid into the face of her former friend, Miss Aomori. She is no longer the most beautiful girl in Aomori Prefecture, but she did later become a Christian which is how I happen to know the story.

Where had all the sin come from in the lives of these two beautiful girls who were such good friends? On one occasion, Jesus was explaining to the Jews that the things which defiled people were not the things they ate, but all the evil and wicked ideas that arose from indwelling sin in the personality.

What comes out of a man is what makes him unclean. For from within, out of men's hearts, come evil thoughts, sexual immorality, theft, murder, adultery, greed, malice, deceit, lewdness, envy, slander, arrogance and folly. All these evils come from inside and make a man unclean (Mark 7: 20–22).

The sins of envy and pride shown in the lives of the two beautiful girls are both mentioned here by Jesus. They illustrate some of the unpleasant things that lurk in the dark places of even the most respectable human heart. I still remember as a schoolboy reading Wells, Huxley and Wells' book *The Science of Life* and, in the interesting section on psychology, there was a picture of a very respectable man walking along the street. Underneath it was another picture of all the evil thoughts and desires running around in that man's unconscious mind or, perhaps, sometimes even in his conscious thoughts. I can still remember how disturbed I felt when I realised that this is what Christians mean when they talk about indwelling sin. After all, the most desperate, hardened and evil criminals were once sweet little children. Why is it that a boy will pull his little sister's hair, or the other way round? It isn't normally that they are following their parents' bad example, but it stems from this bias of the personality of which we are speaking.

May I warn you, please, against thinking that when Christians talk about sin, they are talking about a misuse of sexuality. God meant us to find the opposite sex attractive and he made us that way. In talking about sin, I don't want you to be made to feel guilty about your sexuality, which is a gift of your Creator. He invented sex in the first place and even gave it to vegetables! It was God who made man in his own image, and 'male and female created he them'. Of course, if you should misuse or exploit your own or other people's sexuality, that would be a sin, but then so is all selfish exploitation of any kind. There may be sexual sins about which you ought to feel properly guilty, but so you ought about stealing library books, or shoplifting, or saying malicious things to hurt people to their face or running them down with exaggeration or falsehood behind their backs. We ought to feel ashamed and guilty about greed and malice and just thinking of nobody else but ourselves.

But the point that I am making is that sin is not merely these external symptoms, but an underlying sickness of heart. The symptoms may often seem to be minimal in some pleasant people, but the underlying condition is lurking there in each one of us, suppressed for the time being but dormant like a volcano, waiting to erupt as it did with those two Aomori girls.

What these verses say is that, although I am this sinful kind of person, God still loves me and his love is proved by the very fact that though he knows exactly what I am like underneath, he continues to love me.

Powerless

'When we were still powerless'. The same word is sometimes translated helpless. It is a negative word meaning the absence of power.

It is not that we are entirely without ideals and aspirations and desires to be pleasant and even noble people. None of us consciously want to be mean, selfish or wicked. But we find we can't help it. We are powerless to do good, and lack moral strength to fulfil what we intend. Jesus said, 'Everyone who sins is a slave to sin' (John 8: 34). We soon find ourselves helpless to deliver ourselves. If we use our free will to sin, we soon lose it. We tell one lie and it becomes easier to tell more lies until, in the end, we scarce know truth from falsehood. If we deliberately foster impurity in our thoughts, we can become so defiled that we can't think cleanly even when we want to. We probably all know people who read sniggering innuendos into the simplest statements. Nothing is clean and innocent. We say that they have 'dirty' minds.

It is this helplessness which is part of what theologians call 'total depravity'. Total depravity is quite different from being totally corrupt. If I add a single drop of cyanide to a

glass of water, it is certainly not a hundred per cent poison,
but all of that water is poisoned and contaminated and we
would be foolish to drink any of it.

I am not suggesting for a moment that everybody is as
wicked as they could possibly be (which is manifestly false),
but that every faculty has been spoilt and distorted and
contaminated by this sinful tendency within. It is not only,
as the words of Jesus we have just looked at say, that these
things come out of us, but that every part of us is affected
by sin.

The mind is affected. We all recognise that if everybody
obeyed the Biblical command, 'Thou shalt love thy neigh-
bour as thyself', it would be bound to lead logically to a
much better and happier society. But although my mind
tells me that, I see no point in being the first person to start.

I was amused the other day to see a cartoon of two
prosperous-looking gentlemen standing underneath an
enormous stuffed head of a rhinoceros. One man is explaining to the other, 'I had to bag one, Harry, in case this
damned conservation thing doesn't work and they become
extinct.' We may laugh, but it just shows how the effect of
sin upon us is to make us quite irrational.

We may maintain, 'I don't feel very sinful,' and probably
we don't; and probably the most serious symptom of sin is
that our sense of sinfulness is very much reduced. It used to
be said that tuberculosis patients who were dying often had
an altogether false sense of well-being. One of the results of
sin is that we can't recognise it as sin any more.

In training aircrew, aspiring flyers are put into a pressure
chamber and asked to start counting and writing down
numbers as they count. As the air pressure is reduced, so
the amount of oxygen reaching the brain diminishes. The
observers note that the subjects' counting becomes progressively slower, and their writing more and more irregular.
However if the observers suggest over earphones that their
performance is tailing off, the subjects insist that they are
doing perfectly well and functioning normally. The purpose

of the experiment is to show them that one of the symptoms of oxygen lack is a failure to realise that anything is wrong. One of the results of sin is that we cannot recognise it as sin any longer.

The conscience is affected. Now we all realise, of course, that the conscience is not absolute anyway, and varies very much with our education and upbringing and early training in family and society.

You may know the Flanders and Swann song about the reluctant cannibal, who suddenly says, 'I don't eat people, I won't eat people. I don't eat people. Eating people is wrong!' He is finally talked out of it by his father who, having tried all sorts of other arguments, finally says, 'You might as well say, Don't fight people,' to which he responds, 'Don't fight people? Don't fight . . . ? Ridiculous!'

Consciences are very relative then, but none the less everybody's conscience seems to react at some point, even though the exact point varies considerably with the background and sensitivity of the person concerned. Habitual lying, cheating and stealing can so harden and desensitise a conscience that it functions less and less and can manage only an occasional feeble protest. When a person becomes a Christian, the conscience has to be resensitised and recalibrated against God's standards, rather than the relative standards of contemporary society. But it is surely a matter of common human experience that persistent sinning impairs the ability of the conscience to react and protest.

The will is affected. This is why Paul describes unforgiven sinners as being 'weak' or 'helpless'. The will is so affected that the sinner lacks moral power to resist temptation or to live up to his sincere good intentions, even when he still has any. Paul writes about this when he says,

> I do not understand my own actions. For I do not do what I want, but I do the very thing I hate. Now if I do what I do not want, I agree that the law is good. So

then it is no longer I that do it, but sin which dwells
within me. For I know that nothing good dwells within
me, that is, in my flesh. I can will what is right, but
I cannot do it. For I do not do the good I want, but
the evil I do not want is what I do (Rom.7: 15–19,
RSV).

There can be few people who do not want to do good and
intend to do good, but all of us face this constant problem of
our lack of willpower to do what we believe to be right and
even to live up to our own moral standards, no matter how
far we succeed in lowering them.

The affections are affected. The chief problem about sin is
that we like it. Jesus said, 'Men loved darkness instead of
light because their deeds were evil' (John 3: 19).

In Japanese Kabuki, which is a kind of grand opera, a
very common device is the beautiful princess who waylays
the hero in a forest and allures him. Then there is the
remarkable transformation scene, when she suddenly turns
round and is revealed as being a hideous witch or ogress.
But the blinded hero still thinks she is beautiful. Sin involves the affections, so that we are loath to give up our sin,
as a glutton finds it hard to give up his food or a drunkard
his bottle. I still remember a debate in which a president of
the Oxford Union simpered, 'These Christians ask us if we
are troubled with evil thoughts. Most of us rather enjoy
them.' That is precisely the problem under discussion.

The picture then, is that sin affects the mind, so that sin is
no longer recognised as sin, the affections love sin and are
reluctant to give it up, conscience normally fails to register
sin as sin any more and, even if it does, the will is powerless
to resist evil and do good.

Have you, I wonder, ever found yourself seated in a
moving motor car and known yourself to be helpless to stop
it? This picture of being powerless because of sin is like
being in a car with seat-belt jammed, the steering broken,
the brakes failed and the car plunging towards a huge

chasm, surrounded on all sides by a mass of other traffic, in
which all the other drivers are equally helpless and unable
to escape. The remarkable thing is that while I was still
helpless, God loved me and sent Christ to die for me.

Ungodly

'Christ died for the ungodly.' We live in a society which acts
as though there is no God, which is ungrateful and which
disregards its Creator. Isaiah, when he saw a vision of the
holiness of God, cried out 'I am a man of unclean lips, and I
live among a people of unclean lips.'

What does it mean to be 'ungodly': Paul obviously uses it
to mean something different from 'sinners'. It stresses how
unlike God we are, and how far short of his expectations
for us. My love is chiefly for myself. I certainly find the
command of the Bible that man should love God with
all his heart, mind, soul and strength far too demanding.
I even resent God's totalitarian claim on me: and all those
resentful feelings show that I am indeed 'ungodly'. It is
all that old writers meant when they said someone was
'profane'.

However even though I am 'ungodly' the remarkable
thing is that God still insists on loving me, and it is this
persistence which demonstrates the reality of his love.

Enemies

'When we were God's enemies'. The unbelieving person
feels alienated and hostile to God. It is not that God is
actually threatening us, but that we feel threatened. God
says, 'You shall have no other gods beside me,' we say 'Why
shouldn't I?' We resent God telling us what we may and
may not do. We may not even want to disobey particularly,
but we don't like to be told, so we defy God and assert
ourselves against him. We are antagonistic to him because
he is the enemy of the sin we love.

Men and women need to repent and be converted,
because they have been resentful and hostile, wickedly and

wilfully in rebellion against God. We must lay down the
arms of our rebellion and surrender. What is so astonishing
is that God continues to love us, even though we may be in
open revolt against him. Again we see how different is
God's love from ours.

It is sometimes suggested that people should be converted
because it is to their advantage to become Christians: 'Do
you want joy and peace, prosperity and success?' Such an
approach is using people's selfish motives and encouraging
them to believe that they can use God as a convenience just
to get the things they want.

We are not such pleasant people, then, in God's eyes. We
don't deserve to be loved like this. We scorn God, deny him,
defy him, disobey and disregard him, and many of us live
our lives as though there were no God. God demonstrates
and proves his love by loving us when we are helpless,
ungodly sinners who resent him and are hostile to him.

When we love ourselves least and think that nobody else
could love us – God does. The very name Jesus is derived
from the word meaning 'to save' and, on page one of the
New Testament, where we meet this name for the first time,
we also meet the first reference to sin: 'You are to give him
the name Jesus, because he will save his people from their
sins' (Matt. 1: 21). Jesus came to save us from our sins
because although we are sinners, and God knows we are, he
still loves us.

Now, I have spent a good deal of time on the subject of sin
not because Christians are holier-than-thou sort of people,
or because Christians feel that they're better than anybody
else (God forbid, for you cannot become a Christian at all
without accepting in the first place that you are a sinner and
confessing that you need Jesus to save you from your sins).
But the reason that I have concentrated on this is that many
people express their apathy by saying, 'I feel no need of
Christianity: and I don't need a Saviour.' If we admit that
we are sinners, we are one step nearer to seeing that we
need Jesus to save us.

However, it is all very well to describe the kind of people that God has chosen to love, and we manifestly do not deserve it, but in what way has he proved or demonstrated that he really does love such people? That is the subject of the next chapter.

Chapter 4

THE SAVIOUR OF THE UNGRATEFUL

It may be a cliché to say that God loves, but this needs proving, and has to be demonstrated to a sceptical enquirer who needs to be convinced. After all, how can a Supreme Being, Creator of the whole universe of galaxies be said to love a pathetic creature who lives to see only some seventy summers? The parties seem too disparate for the relationship to be meaningful. As we have already shown, the objects of God's love are unresponsive, even hostile and morally unattractive.

HOW DOES GOD LOVE MAN?

Human beings hint at love by sending unsigned Valentine cards. The purpose of the unsigned Valentine is to arouse the curiosity of the recipient – who on earth could have sent it? God the Creator and Provider showers joys and gifts indiscriminately upon mankind. The Bible expresses this as 'He causes his sun to rise on the evil and the good' (Matt. 5: 45). The mother holding her baby up in the air, while he wriggles and laughs with her, enjoys her child. The father enjoying a walk and talk with his child feels the wonder of relationship, and unexpressed affection. But this is something that the Creator gives quite indiscriminately – believers and unbelievers alike share in these human delights. In the one case there is a sense of thankfulness to God, in the other no sense of gratitude at all. In this wider and general sense God is the Saviour of the ungrateful, and the Bible comments that God is 'the Saviour of all men, and especially of those who believe' (I Tim. 4: 10).

But the giving of presents by men to women, saying it with flowers or with chocolates, is a token that says that ultimately I want to give myself to you and for you to give yourself to me. While certainly, because we are merely human, this loving and self-giving may be selfish and incomplete, it is wonderfully, one of the highest expressions of which human love is capable.

God, who has showered all men, evil and good, indiscriminately with the gifts of his common grace, has also given his Son for us and the Son has given himself on our behalf. As Paul called him 'the Son of God, who loved me and gave himself for me' (Gal. 2: 20). But why should Christ dying on the cross be thought to have such significance?

Does the fact that Christ died leave you cold? Does it seem irrelevant? Well, you reply, how does a man dying on a cross in Jerusalem two thousand years ago help me now? It does not seem to have any direct relationship with my present experience. Suppose for a moment that I told you that somebody had dived into a nearby river in order to demonstrate their love for you. It seems a rather pointless exercise. But suppose that you had fallen into that river, were too weak to swim out of its strong current, and were drowning . . . and that somebody came in after you, and rescued you and others at the cost of their own life, you would have no problem over relevance, and you would be grateful. The previous chapter was concerned to show that we do have a problem, that we are in peril as alienated sinners, and so need to be rescued and saved.

I have always been moved by Sidney Carter's song called 'Friday Morning' in which the dying thief on the cross next to Jesus recognises that the carpenter does not deserve to die, and says that everything is to be blamed upon God. Ignorant of who Jesus is, and the irony of his own words, he says:

> It's God they ought to crucify
> Instead of you and me,
> I said unto the carpenter
> A-hanging on the tree.

The Bible says that God was in Christ reconciling us to himself, allowing him to be crucified instead of you and me. This is why Romans 5 says that God has proved his love towards us because while we were still alienated sinners, Christ died for us.

The New Testament uses at least four major illustrations to explain the meaning of the death of Christ, to explain how it is that his death is significant for us today. In some places the Bible uses one set of language, in another place another group, and sometimes it uses several illustrations together.

Firstly, it uses the language of *human relationships*. 'For if when we were God's enemies, we were reconciled to him through the death of his Son, how much more, having been reconciled, shall we be saved through his life!' (Rom. 5: 10). We have been 'enemies', alienated and estranged from God, rebels who have grievously offended him. But now he has taken a peace initiative (we are still hostile, remember) and has declared an amnesty, and we have to decide whether to be reconciled or not.

Secondly, it uses the language of the *law court*. 'Since we have now been justified by his blood, how much more shall we be saved from God's wrath through him!' (Rom. 5: 9). The word 'justified' is legal language. Guilty offenders against the moral laws stand before the judge who himself accepts the penalty that the law demands of us. The guilty sinner is justified. Paul uses this illustration particularly in the letter to the Romans.

Thirdly, there is the language of *temple sacrifice*, used in the words 'by his blood'. This is the language of the temple ritual, and sees Christ acting on the cross both as priest, through his eternal divine nature, and the sacrifice, through his human mortal nature. We are cleansed and purified from our sins because the substitute victim has been put to death in our place.

Fourthly, though not used here, there is the language of the *slave market*, a vivid picture which Jesus himself used when he said he had come to 'give his life as a ransom for many' (Mark 10: 45). The cross is seen as the means by which we are liberated from slavery.

As in the passage we have been looking at, these different explanations are often combined.

It cannot be overemphasised that Christ is not showing his love in a vague and uncertain way which merely causes the subjective response of love in us. It is not simply that we are *subjectively* moved. It is very clear from this passage (and many others) that Christ achieved something *objective* when he reconciled rebels, justified offenders and sacrificed his blood to atone for sinful worshippers and liberate oppressed slaves. The bridge between hostile sinners and a loving God is the cross of Jesus.

I well remember when I first began to grasp this. I went to a school where there was very little in daily chapel that was helpful, except in the hymns we sang. Enthusiastic religion was then regarded by headmasters as emotional and not quite respectable.

For my part, I was trying to be 'good', but not doing very well at it. I had somehow gained the false impression that today's good deeds could be set in the accounts against yesterday's failures. Unfortunately, my sense of sinfulness steadily increased, and I never seemed to achieve enough good to offset very much of the accumulation of unforgiven sins. I was praying that God would forgive me for the sins of today, yesterday and the day before yesterday, because I hoped that I might do some good tomorrow.

And, finally, the penny dropped that some of the hymns that we were singing provided the answer for my troubled conscience; 'He died that we might be forgiven' meant that the only grounds on which God would forgive me were that

Christ had died for me. It was no good my hoping to atone for my failures with my own good deeds – 'Nothing in my hand I bring'. I could not atone for my sins with my own good deeds – 'O Saviour I have naught to plead, Except my own exceeding need, And thy exceeding love'.

HELL FIRE AND ALL THAT

People naturally shrink from the hell-fire sandwich-board approach to Christianity. However, one of the very interesting things about this passage we have been looking at in Romans is that, while it talks about the pouring out of God's love and the proof of God's love, it also talks about wrath – we 'shall be saved from God's wrath through him!'

How can a God of love also be a God of wrath? Christians can hardly mean that God is bad tempered?

Some have offered the facile suggestion that the God of the Old Testament is a God of wrath and the God of the New Testament a God of love. This just does not hold water, for the Old Testament has some moving statements about God's love and the New Testament some very powerful passages about God's wrath. And we do not resolve this problem merely by ignoring wrath. If we do we shall have a very inadequate, lopsided and unbiblical view of what God is like.

God hates sin and evil: he cannot tolerate, excuse or condone it. We ought not to confuse wrath with outbursts of human bad temper, any more than we confuse God's love with selfish, fickle and changeable human love.

Wrath may be described as God's unchanging, implacable and sustained hatred of sin. Even the smallest drop of water dropped into concentrated sulphuric acid will cause it to explode violently. That antipathy is a fixed property of the acid. So also does holiness have the inevitable reaction of wrath whenever it encounters sin.

This may be illustrated in all sorts of different ways.

Legal authorities cannot overlook or condone crime. Health authorities can react in either of two different ways towards disease. Either they must destroy it and stamp it out or, alternatively, they must isolate it. Animals infected with rabies must either be destroyed or isolated: they cannot be allowed to roam freely wherever they will, infecting others with their horrible disease.

Both of these categories are found in the Bible: that is to say, destroying fire and the isolation of outer darkness. Sinners could not possibly be allowed into heaven untreated, for if they were, it would very quickly cease to be heaven. And so the teaching of Jesus makes it very clear that the same two categories are to deal with sin: namely, exposure to his wrath and exclusion from his presence.

The wrath of God is described in the New Testament both as a present process and a future judgment. Thus, we are told 'The wrath of God is being revealed from heaven against all the godlessness and wickedness of men, who suppress the truth by their wickedness' (Rom. 1: 18). And later on in that same chapter, three times we are told that 'God gave them over' (Rom. 1: 24, 26, 28). Thus wrath is seen as a present reality. The universe is arranged in such a way, as a fixed property, that sinful behaviour produces inevitable miserable consequences. From our daily newspapers, we see the misery of marital unfaithfulness leading to unhappiness, broken homes, disturbed children and divorce.

Other verses reveal that the wrath of God is also being stored up against the future: 'Because of your stubbornness and your unrepentant heart, you are storing up wrath against yourself for the day of God's wrath' (Rom. 2: 5).

Our memory for the sins we have committed is often pretty brief, although our consciences seem, in fact, to record our failures much as the black box in an aircraft makes a record of the journey travelled. In the mountains of Aomori, on some of the country roads, they were still using horse-drawn carts. Each day, the horses would cross over the pass,

dirtying the road with their droppings. But during the night
snow would fall and the road would be white and clean
again until, once again, the horses crossed the path and the
snow was stained by the horse manure. But again, the snow
would fall, night by night, and all would be well until the
spring thaw and then, as the snow melted away, the filthy
condition of the roads was apparent to everybody. In the
same way, we sin but then go off to sleep and, somehow, the
night's sleep seems to obliterate the memory of the failures
of the previous day; and each night's sleep, like the snow,
covers over more moral manure, until the day of reckoning
and of God's judgment comes. We ought not to overlook
the fact that the Bible teaches frankly about this, though we
should notice at once that it does this as a gentle admoni-
tion to repent and to show a change of heart.

> Therefore you have no excuse, O man, whoever you
> are, when you judge another; for in passing judgment
> upon him you condemn yourself, because you, the
> judge, are doing the very same things. We know that
> the judgment of God rightly falls upon those who do
> such things. Do you suppose, O man, that when you
> judge those who do such things and yet do them your-
> self, you will escape the judgment of God? Or do you
> presume upon the riches of his kindness and for-
> bearance and patience? Do you not know that God's
> kindness is meant to lead you to repentance? But by your
> hard and impenitent heart you are storing up wrath for
> yourself on the day of wrath when God's righteous
> judgment will be revealed (Rom. 2: 1–5, RSV).

These two elements of exposure to God's wrath and
exclusion from God's presence are both hinted at in the
gospel accounts of the death of Christ. In Gethsemane,
Christ prayed, 'If it is possible, may this cup be taken from
me' (Matt. 26: 39). The prophets, Isaiah, Jeremiah and
Ezekiel and the book of Revelation all speak of a cup of

wrath which has to be drunk: Jesus saved us from the wrath of God by drinking it up himself.

Again, on the cross at Calvary, Jesus quoted Psalm 22, 'My God, my God, why have you forsaken me?' The cry of a man who felt excluded from God's presence. Because of our sin, we deserve alienation and exclusion from God's presence: Jesus experienced that God-forsakenness on our behalf. As the Bible puts it, he tasted death for everyone (Heb. 2: 9).

We cannot guess what it meant for the holy Son of God to bear the defilement and disgrace of our sin.

I was talking once with a woman whose husband had been seriously disgraced. Trying to comfort her, I said that she was surely better off than another woman whose missionary husband had recently been murdered in Thailand. I have never forgotten her reply. 'I think I envy her,' she said. The other woman had lost her husband, but he had died in honour. Her husband was still living, but she was bearing the stigma and agony of her husband's failure and shame.

It is possible for one person's sin and failure seriously to affect the lives of others, so that they suffer because of it too. Jesus was suffering not just for one person's sins, but for the sins of all sinners. And not only for sinners in general, but for me in particular.

Can you, I wonder, grasp the idea that God's love has been demonstrated to you personally? Each of us can say, as Paul said, that he 'loved me and gave himself for me' (Gal. 2: 20).

We have barely an inkling of the terrible God-forsakenness of men without God. The Lord Jesus bore its full weight for me, so that I need never know it. It's when we begin to realise that his death has obtained for us reconciliation with God, forgiveness of our sin, cleansing of our guilt and release from our slavery, then to begin to understand how much he has loved us.

UNREQUITED LOVE?

Love can be joyously accepted or sullenly refused. We may spurn, reject and 'cold shoulder' the love God demonstrated in sending his Son to die for us. We may disregard that death as wasted, worthless and of no interest, or we may respond to God's love as Paul did and experience that 'the love of God has been poured out into our hearts . . .'

There are only two classes of people reading this book: those who have responded to the love of God and those who are still rejecting it.

I don't know whether you ever have the kind of ludicrous thought that I sometimes have at a wedding ceremony. The bridegroom has responded to the question, 'Do you take this woman' and has made his vows and said that he will take her 'from that day forward, for richer for poorer, in sickness and in health'. Then the minister turns and this time addresses his question to the woman: 'Will you take this man . . .' I've often wondered what would happen if, having reached that point, she couldn't make up her mind. I stand there holding my breath to see whether the girl will reply or not!

God has made his intentions absolutely clear. He has declared his love in a most unequivocal way and said that he would accept us, and has promised to take us and look after us for ever. He has made his promises and now he waits for us to respond.

It's not enough for us to approve of God, or to patronise him by coming to church occasionally, as though we were doing him a favour. It's as though the woman replied, 'Well, if you want me to, I'll come and visit you now and again, and I'll think about you sometimes.' God is not so much interested in our promises to come to church more frequently, or to live a better life. 'No,' he says, 'it's you I want.' I love the quotation from *Christ the Tiger* – 'Give me the worship of your heart, *your heart* and be merry and thankful and lowly and not pompous and gaunt and sere.'[1]

The God who loves us, wants us, and wants our love in return.

And so I ask you: Will you take this Jesus to be your Lord and Saviour and, forsaking all others, cleave only unto him?

But, before you say 'I will', remember that taking vows at a wedding isn't something you just do and then go back to the old life. It's the beginning of a new life, with a new allegiance, it means a complete change of timetable and lifestyle and commitment to another person.

Nor is it normally something private and secret, but it is something which is done publicly, so that everybody knows that from now on the two of you belong together. The Prayer Book marriage service used to say that this is not something to be done 'unadvisedly and wantonly'. While emotion may accompany marriage, we don't get married because of emotion.

And only when we have weighed up very carefully whether indeed we wish to give our lives to God and to live for him do we say 'I will'. So don't rush into becoming a Christian, unless you are prepared for that kind of wholehearted commitment and change of lifestyle.

Chapter 5

THE PRINCE WHO GIVES LIFE

In our opening chapter we saw some of the remarkable descriptions of 'the Son' given by the writer to the Hebrews. We have also thought of him as God come 'down to earth', and as one who died on the cross so that the sins of mankind might be forgiven. However we now need to look more closely at Jesus of Nazareth, and at the identification we have been making of him with the Son of God come 'down to earth'. This is a cardinal belief of historic Christianity, but would be questioned both by Jews and Muslims. In this next section we want to examine afresh the grounds for this Christian conviction.

There was a day not long after the apostles had first met Jesus when, in their home town of Capernaum in their native Galilee, Jesus was speaking to a packed house. Suddenly he was interrupted by a commotion – the roof was opened up and four men let a paralysed man down in front of Jesus, because they wanted him to be healed. Everybody held their breath. What would Jesus do? Would he heal him?

Jesus at once angered the scribes, the Jewish teachers, by saying, 'Friend, your sins are forgiven.' All Jews believed that forgiving sins was a divine prerogative: 'Who can forgive sins but God alone?' Jesus's next statement was a deliberate challenge to this hostile reaction: 'Which is easier: to say, "Your sins are forgiven," or to say, "Get up and walk"?'

There was a pause while everybody thought about it. Then Jesus continued, 'That you may know that the Son of

Man has authority on earth to forgive sins,' he said to the paralytic, 'I tell you, get up, take your mat and go home' (Luke 5: 17–26).

So Jesus did the apparently more difficult thing of getting this man visibly walking. But the healing was intended as a sign demonstrating that Jesus also had the authority to forgive sins. However if forgiving sins, in Jewish thinking, was a prerogative of the One God alone, it raised the crucial question of the identity of Jesus of Nazareth. Who does he think he is?

Some time later, after Jesus had died, risen and ascended, there were new miracles. The gospel accounts portray the apostles as cowards, cynics and fugitives, who all ran away when he was arrested (Mark 14: 50), and refused to believe the story of the women that the tomb was empty and that angels announced he had risen from the dead (Luke 24: 11). And now, here are those same men, walking calmly into those same temple courts where Jesus had been teaching and his enemies had been plotting only two months earlier:

> One day Peter and John were going up to the temple at the time of prayer – at three in the afternoon. Now a man crippled from birth was being carried to the temple gate called Beautiful, where he was put every day to beg from those going into the temple courts. When he saw Peter and John about to enter, he asked them for money. Peter looked straight at him, as did John. Then Peter said, 'Look at us!' So the man gave them his attention, expecting to get something from them. Then Peter said, 'Silver and gold I do not have, but what I have I give to you. In the name of Jesus Christ of Nazareth walk.' Taking him by the right hand, he helped him up, and instantly the man's feet and ankles became strong. He jumped to his feet and began to walk. Then he went into the temple courts, walking and jumping, and praising God (Acts 3: 1–8).

How does one account for this transformation? It is hard to explain it, apart from the resurrection of Jesus. Having transformed his followers, he transforms this helpless beggar through them.

Luke, the author of the book of Acts, and the doctor, describes with clinical interest the congenital lameness and the strengthening of the man's feet and ankle bones. But this passage really asks to be danced by a skilful dancer. You can almost sense the man's incredulity and delight as, for the first time in his life, he stands on his feet and realises that his legs are supporting him, and then he begins to walk and then to leap and one Japanese translation of this story has him 'Leaping and dancing'.

But this also was a sign. The prophet Isaiah had prophesied of the messianic age: 'Then will the eyes of the blind be opened and the ears of the deaf unstopped. Then will *the lame leap like a deer*, and the tongue of the dumb shout for joy' (Isa. 35: 5–6, my italics). And now here it was happening again! Peter takes this opportunity of the excited crowd gathering together to explain the resurrection of Jesus as the fulfilling of what the Old Testament prophets had predicted.

In Matthew 11 Jesus likened himself to a piper calling others to dance, and he certainly changed miserable men's mourning into dancing during his lifetime.

Interestingly, Nietzsche once said, 'I should believe only in a God who understood how to dance.'[1]

So, what does this sign mean? It means, as Peter later declared (Acts 3: 15) that Jesus is the Prince of Life who transforms lives. It seems probable that the lame man had never been in through the Beautiful Gate into the temple before. The law forbade any man with a defect from being a priest, and those who were lame or deformed were excluded from the sanctuary (Lev. 21: 18). He certainly could not have gone in by himself and it looks as though his friends carried him only as far as the steps. But now, he goes in with the apostles to worship and enters his courts with thanksgiving and his gates with praise. The whining beggar has become a dancing worshipper. In the temple worship they sang the Psalms, including the one which says, 'You turned my wailing into dancing; you removed my sackcloth and clothed me with joy' (Ps. 30: 11).

But the story that delights me most is when Jesus goes to the tomb of Lazarus. The Prince of Life opens graves and

> Lazarus from the tomb advancing,
> Once more drew life's sweet breath.
> You too will leave the churchyard dancing
> For I have conquered death.[2]

While I was in Oxford recently, I made a point of visiting New College Chapel to see Epstein's statue of Lazarus, with the grave-cloth bandages slipping off him. This is what Christ does for people!

A woman chronically ill for years touches the hem of his robe and his life floods into her. Everybody kept well clear of people with leprosy, lest they be contaminated and ceremonially defiled. But Jesus deliberately touches the leper whom nobody would have touched since his childhood, and the life of Jesus floods in to the man and washes him clean.

Doesn't this grab you?

But, back to our incident at the Beautiful Gate. We have thought about the apostles and we have thought of the beggar, but this account also draws our attention to the spectators.

> When all the people saw him walking and praising God they recognised him as the same man who used to sit begging at the temple gate called Beautiful, and they were filled with wonder and amazement at what had happened to him. While the beggar held on to Peter and John, all the people were astonished and came running to them in the place called Solomon's Colonnade (Acts 3: 9–11).

If you have ever seen a life transformed by Christ, it makes you wonder.

In my first term at college, another member of the College XV was converted. He lived over the Little Rose in Trumpington Street, was often drunk, though I suspect that somebody was exaggerating when they told me that he knew more dirty stories than the rest of the college put together. But in November of that year, Colin was soundly converted through the power of Jesus. It so happened that a number of other members of the team were meeting in the room next to mine for what I can only describe as a panic meeting, and I overheard one of the other forwards protesting that 'If a man like Colin can get converted, none of us are safe!'

The people in the temple were filled with wonder and amazement. They were attracted by what Jesus had done and yet, perhaps as we are sometimes, fearful of enjoying that experience for themselves. Peter and John were quite ready to grab the opportunity: this man was a living example of what the name of Jesus could do if people trusted in him. And so they began to speak to the crowd.

> When Peter saw this, he said to them: 'Men of Israel, why does this surprise you? Why do you stare at us as if by our own power or godliness we had made this man walk? The God of Abraham, Isaac and Jacob, the God of our fathers, has glorified his servant Jesus. You handed him over to be killed, and you disowned him before Pilate, though he had decided to let him go. You disowned the Holy and Righteous One and asked that a murderer be released to you. You killed the author of life, but God raised him from the dead. We are witnesses of this. By faith in the name of Jesus this man whom you see and know was made strong. It is Jesus' name and the faith that comes through him that has given this complete healing to him, as you can all see . . . This is how God fulfilled what he had foretold through

all the prophets, saying that his Christ would suffer . . .
Indeed, all the prophets from Samuel on, as many as
have spoken, have foretold these days (Acts 3: 12–24).

Recently, a tribal group in Nigeria, called the Maguzawa,
have noted what the shepherd in Jesus's parable did when
he found his sheep and what the woman did when she found
her coin. They called together their neighbours for a feast,
to join them in rejoicing (Luke 15). People often think that
when people become Christians they will isolate themselves
from their neighbours and move into some Christian ghetto.
But the Maguzawa hold a party and call together their
neighbours for a feast, to rejoice with them. The convert
wants to celebrate his conversion with his friends and tell
them that now he is a Christian he is, in fact, commanded to
love his neighbours. And one such feast leads to another, as
others attracted by the change also put their faith in Christ.

As the lame man is so manifestly rejoicing and delighted
at what Christ has done for him, Peter and John expect that
others will start rejoicing. Perhaps you have seen one of
your own friends converted and you have been surprised.
You have watched and waited to see whether that change
has been real and lasting, and perhaps the reason that you
are now reading this book is that you are trying to find
out for yourself whether Jesus is real and can make you
real.

Some months earlier than the healing of the lame man,
Jesus had also attracted a crowd in the very same area of
the temple in Jerusalem. The Jews had gathered round him
and said, 'How long will you keep us in suspense? If you are
the Christ, tell us plainly.' Jesus chides them for not believing in spite of all the miracles and 'signs' he had performed;
the credentials of his messiahship. And then he concludes
by saying, 'I and the Father are one' (John 10: 30). It is
clear that they did not understand this to be a pious statement of unity with God which anybody might make, for
they immediately took up stones to stone him. When he

asked 'For which of [my good works] do you stone me?', they replied, 'For blasphemy, because you, a mere man, claim to be God.' The same reason was given again at his trial in explanation to Pilate: 'We have a law, and according to that law he must die because he claimed to be the Son of God' (John 19: 7). This is the issue which all of us must face: is Jesus who he claimed to be or not?

It is very easy for us to fail to appreciate the force of Jesus's statements like, 'I am the bread of life', 'I am the good shepherd' and so on. We may not realise that 'I am' is God's name. When Moses asked what name he should give to Pharaoh, God replied, 'I am who I am,' and 'This is what you are to say to the Israelites: "I AM has sent me to you"' (Ex. 3: 14).

The personal name of God, Yahweh (usually translated as 'Lord' in our Bibles), is also thought to be derived from the verb *hawah*, which means 'to be'. God is the only self-existent being. He is not a contingent being like ourselves, dependent for our existence upon other human beings and upon God himself. But God is self-existent, and does not depend for his own existence upon any other being outside of himself.

Some languages are able to express the respective status or the dignity of a speaker by the pronoun that is used. There is the respectful 'Sie' and the more familiar 'Du' used for the second person singular in German, where in modern English we merely say 'you'. In a respect language like Japanese, there are a whole row of different first person singular pronouns for 'I'. But there is one word for 'I' which is used only by the emperor himself: 'Chin'. It's his own very personal pronoun. If you hear somebody say 'Chin' about themselves, then that person is either the emperor or somebody who is under the mistaken impression that he is the emperor! In a rather similar way, the expression 'I am' is the name of God and can be used only by God of himself. Thus, for example, in saying 'I am the good shepherd', Jesus is referring back to Ezekiel 34, where the Lord promises explicitly that he himself will come to be the shepherd of his own people. In using the pronoun which only God uses of himself, Jesus is making a direct claim to divinity.

This is significantly illustrated in the conversion of the apostle Paul. When, on the road to Damascus he asked, 'Who are you, Lord?', the solemn reply came, 'I am Jesus, whom you are persecuting' (Acts 26: 15). This throws considerable light on Paul's conversion. It is as though the answer to his question, 'Who are you?' is simply, 'Yahweh, Jesus'.

You cannot honestly read the gospels without facing the claims Jesus makes for himself. Jesus is repeatedly taking God's name as his own, accepting men's worship and forgiving men's sins.

What is so remarkable is what somebody has called Jesus' *'holy egocentricity'* – that is to say that he is for ever contrasting his own status with that of all other men and proposing himself as the One and only solution to all of their problems. The following simple propositions from the gospels make this clear. Jesus, in effect, says:

'You men are all sinners; I am not only not a sinner but I have come specifically in order to save sinners.

'You men are all sick; and I am not only not sick, but I am the Great Physician who has come to heal you.

'You men are all lost sheep; I am not only not a lost sheep, but I have come as the Good Shepherd to seek and save that which is lost.

'Your lives are all forfeit because of sin; my life is not only not forfeit, but I have come in order to give my life as a ransom for sinners.'[3]

What other man could so challenge a group of strict adherents to the Jewish Law, determined if at all possible to find fault in him? For that matter, what man would make such a claim as that to his own close friends who knew him best? If you or I were to make claims like that, the members of our own family or all those who knew us best would surely laugh at us.

One interesting feature of the New Testament is that the longer this small intimate circle of men knew Jesus, the more ready they were to accept his sensational claims. We should remember also who they were. These were not superstitious Greeks, ready to accept the whole pantheon of extremely anthropomorphic gods and goddesses, but Jews who, like Jesus, had been brought up from childhood as fanatical monotheists. It is a fact of history that the Roman legions left their eagle standards at Caesarea and marched into Jerusalem without them. The Jews regarded the eagles as idolatrous and, on one occasion, bare-handed Jewish civilians had fought against heavily armed Roman troops rather than allow these idols into their holy city. For a Jew to believe that the carpenter of Nazareth was the Son of God come in the flesh ran counter to their whole religious upbringing. It is not surprising in itself that Jesus had a following of people who believed in him, for so have many cranks and charlatans in the course of history. What is significant is that such men (fanatical, monotheistic Jews) should have believed such a thing (that a man was the Son of God come in the flesh) of such a man (a provincial carpenter from Galilee).

One sometimes hears people say that all they wish to retain of the New Testament is the Sermon on the Mount, which they seem content to regard as a few ethical directions for life. People who say that have obviously overlooked entirely the explicit and implicit claims made by Jesus about himself within that very sermon. Jesus is prepared to say, 'Blessed are you when people insult you, persecute you and falsely say all kinds of evil against you *because of me*' (Matt. 5: 11, my italics). What is a Galilean carpenter saying about himself when he says, 'Do not think that I have come to abolish the Law or the Prophets; I have not come to abolish them but to fulfil them. I tell you the truth, until heaven and earth disappear, not the smallest letter, not the least stroke of a pen, will by any means disappear from the Law until everything is accomplished' (Matt. 5: 17–18).

Why should the Law and the prophets, which every Jew regarded as the very Word of God, require the authentication of this carpenter? Or again, 'Not everyone who says to me, "Lord, Lord," will enter the kingdom of heaven, but only he who does the will of my Father who is in heaven. Many will say to me on that day, "Lord, Lord, did we not prophesy in your name, and in your name drive out demons, and perform many miracles?" Then I will tell them plainly, "I never knew you. Away from me, you evildoers!" (Matt. 7: 21–23). Jesus is claiming that on that final day of judgment what is going to matter more than anything else is that people know him.

The final parable of the wise man who builds his house upon the rock compared with the foolish man who builds upon the sand is that 'everyone who hears these words of *mine*, and puts them into practice is like a wise man who built his house on the rock . . . But everyone who hears these words of *mine* and does not put them into practice is like a foolish man who built his house on sand' (Matt. 7: 24–26, my italics). No wonder the people who listened to him were amazed at his teaching, because he taught with such authority. Jesus, in the Sermon on the Mount, says that his words are foundational for human living.

What, then, are we to believe about Jesus? Is it credible to believe that he was a deliberate fraud and charlatan who knew that his own claims were rubbish but deliberately went about trying to deceive people? Does that really tie in with the things that he did?

Or, on the other hand, are we to believe that Jesus suffered from megalomania and that, while utterly sincere, he was thoroughly deluded . . . in a very nice way? But, again, is this credible and, if so, why on earth should anybody ever have believed in him?

The most beautiful descriptions are given to us of this Jesus who first taught his followers in Solomon's Portico. John says that he was 'full of grace and truth' (John 1: 14). The multitude were utterly astonished and said, 'He has

done everything well' (Mark 7: 37). Luke reports that he
made a deep impression on his first hearers who were
'amazed at the gracious words that came from his lips'
(Luke 4: 22). The officers sent out to arrest him came back
empty-handed and, when asked to explain why they had
not arrested him, said, 'No-one ever spoke the way this man
does' (John 7: 46).

He had time to spend with racial outcasts like the
Samaritans and would eat at table with social outcasts like
the tax-gatherers and, indeed, made both a Samaritan and
a tax-collector heroes in two of his parables. He held babies
in his arms, took children to sit on his knee and rich men,
poor men, sick men, mad men and women all came to him
for help. And yet this Jesus is no milk and water, stained-
glass window, Gothic Christ. He is the most winsome of all
beings, ready to share that winsomeness with us.

This is the man whom Peter, speaking to the crowd
gathered by Solomon's Portico, calls 'the Prince of Life'.
But then he continues, 'God raised him from the dead. We
are witnesses of this.' The lame man at the Beautiful Gate
is now walking because of the power of the Prince of Life
whom God raised from the dead.

While we are free to argue if we will that the first-century
people were pre-scientific, they were only too well aware
that the Romans were efficient butchers. The people the
Romans executed never came back to life again. These men
were preaching in Jerusalem only a few hundred yards from
where it all happened and only within a very few weeks of it
happening. They could go and see for themselves if the
tomb was empty.

One spring I took the opportunity of being in Jerusalem
myself, to walk from the Wailing Wall (all that is left on the
surface of Herod's Temple) as far as the garden tomb, just
to see how long it would take. It took me only some twelve
minutes of normal walking. If Jesus was safely buried in his
tomb, why weren't these preachers laughed to scorn? Why
was it that so many Jews in Jerusalem became Christians?

Why were they ready to be persecuted and chased out of their homes in Jerusalem and scattered, unless they were absolutely convinced of the truth of the resurrection?

It would take a gifted film director to do justice to that staggering morning when Mary came running to Peter and John and said to them, 'They have taken away the Lord out of the tomb, and we do not know where they have laid Him.' And then these very two men themselves began to run to get to the tomb. John, being the younger man, ran faster and got there first. Peter, as the older man, ran more slowly and arrived panting but, completely in character, went straight into the tomb (John 20: 4–6). John then followed him in and saw the grave clothes in position, but empty, collapsed under the weight of the spices, with the head cloth separated from the body wrappings by the width of a face which is no longer there.

These two preachers at Solomon's Portico were not reporting something second-hand, as I have to do, and as anybody has to do today. They were reporting something they themselves had experienced, seen and lived through.

Peter concludes his message with the exhortation to his hearers, 'Repent, then, and turn to God, so that your sins may be wiped out' (Acts 3: 19).

Can you see yourself as that lame beggar, crippled morally from your birth, sitting outside the temple of God?

Becoming a Christian demands that we confess ourselves to be such moral beggars and spiritual cripples, who need the Prince of Life to lift us up to singing and dancing and leaping and praising God.

A rather amusing drama based on this story has the cripple refusing the efforts of the apostles to change his lifestyle. 'Get off! What do you think I am, some kind of nut-case? Trying to take my living away from me, aren't you? You Jesus people are all the same. Can't slip a guy a few coins like normal people. You want to be changing them and healing them and making them better, don't you! Well, I earn a pretty penny as I am, so just you push off!'[4]

It seems almost incomprehensible to believe that anybody would voluntarily choose to remain a crippled beggar when they could be leaping and dancing. Jesus, the Prince of Life, could bring that transformation into your life as well. He doesn't just want you to admire him and what he can do, but he wants to share his life and vitality with you. He wants to take you by the hand, lift you to your feet, and set you dancing!

Chapter 6

THE INVITED TAKEOVER

In the first five chapters we have concentrated upon Jesus Christ: who he is and what he has done. The Bible says that God has spoken to us through him in a revelation surpassing that of Moses and the prophets, who spoke of his coming. This all suggests that we should take his claims seriously.

Then we learned that the pre-existent Christ deliberately humbled himself in assuming human nature and voluntarily dying, and that in consequence of this God has enthroned him and proclaimed that he is Lord. Therefore he deserves our homage and we should swear our allegiance.

Then we saw that God has proved his love through the death of Jesus on behalf of sinful human beings: such love calls for a response.

Jesus is proclaimed by the apostles as the Prince of Life, who has overcome death in rising from the grave, and wants to share his life with us, so that our mourning is turned into dancing. We should respond by accepting this offered gift of life.

Here is this winsome, attractive person who spoke wonderful words, performed marvellous deeds and made astonishing claims. He then died on the cross, apparently discredited as a liar and deceiver. Seldom in human history could anybody have lost face so suddenly and completely. How could Jews ever respect, let alone believe in, a man executed for blasphemy, that is for claiming to be God? The cross would appear to be the finish of Christianity, because its founder was discredited. However God vindicated him by raising him from the dead and thus, at the same time, authenticating him as his Son whose claims are true and to be accepted. The apostles never tire of saying, 'But God raised him from the dead.'

His death, therefore, was not an accident, a gruesome mistake, an unfortunate oversight, but Jesus was 'handed over to you by God's set purpose and foreknowledge' (Acts 2: 23). This planned death was God's way of dealing with human sin; 'But this is how God fulfilled what he had foretold through all the prophets, saying that his Christ would suffer' (Acts 3: 18). The death of Christ is a God-provided way of cleansing, forgiveness, reconciliation and emancipation.

This, however, raises a fresh question: suppose for a moment that we grant that the claims of the apostles recorded in the New Testament documents show that *Jesus is real in history*, how can all that be *presently relevant to me today?* How can historical events which are alleged to have occurred in Palestine two thousand years ago be relevant to me, living in the world today? We need both reality and relevance. I may claim that my religion (whatever it is) must be true because it works in my subjective experience. This may help me, but it helps nobody else. My subjective experience might well be misled and misplaced. I could well be deceiving myself and, in any case, it is extraordinarily difficult to explain one's subjective experience to other people.

I could also say that I know my beliefs are true because they have an objective basis in historical events. Other people can investigate and examine these things for themselves. A valid religion must have an objective foundation in historical events. But these alone are not enough either, unless they have some relevance in present subjective experience. We must be able to say first that a set of beliefs is true and secondly that they work. Subjective experience is not good unless it rests upon an objective foundation, but the objective foundation is no good unless it can be subjectively realised and its relevance experienced. So, in this chapter, we want to consider the connection between the facts about Jesus Christ which we have been considering and how they relate to the present religious experience of Christians.

First of all, we are faced with the problem of the present invisibility of Jesus.

'Where is he then?' 'Gone back to heaven.' 'Very convenient indeed!' says the sceptic.

One possible reply would be that a creator of the universe, whom you could see visibly within the universe, would be too small to be credible as the creator of it. What would you expect him to look like anyway?

One can imagine the uproar in the theatre when Hamlet is declaiming 'To be or not to be' if a long-haired character walks on to the stage and, when asked who he thinks he might be, he replies 'I am William Shakespeare'. The Christian position is that the creator of the universe has indeed made a unique and significant appearance in the central act of his cosmic drama but that he is not now scheduled to reappear until the closing curtain (see the last chapter). Yet the cynic responds that it seems very convenient to argue for an historical Christ, who is now absent, and whose past appearance cannot be proved and whose future appearance has yet to take place. Why, after all, did he not remain on earth following the resurrection as a permanent proof of the Creator's good will towards all men?

Well, let's suppose for a moment that he had done just that and that with the apostles he had set up a shrine of some kind in Jerusalem, so that pilgrims could come and visit him, and satisfy themselves of the truth of Christianity. We would have established, if you like, a kind of Christian equivalent of the Muslim pilgrimage to Mecca. However, instead of going to kiss the black stone which Mohammed kissed, one would be able to go and meet Jesus in the flesh. So, if any of us wanted to satisfy ourselves about the truth of Christianity, all we would need to do would be to save up

enough money to take ship to Haifa or fly charter to Tel
Aviv. When we arrived there, however, we would find huge
crowds and long queues. This might well be wonderful
for Israel's tourist industry, but would probably provide
a further major feeding problem for the United Nations.
Planes and ships packed with pilgrims would be pouring
into Israel much faster than pilgrims could be processed
through the audience chamber, even assuming around-the-
clock interviews. After a very long and patient wait there
would be time for perhaps only a thirty-second interview.
We would certainly know that Christian belief was true, but
all that we would have left afterwards would be a treasured
memory of an unforgettable experience. Jesus would certainly be real, but not really very relevant for the remainder
of my earthly life. His presence in Jerusalem might convince
the sceptical (or would they still suspect some trick?) of the
truth of the resurrection, but it would not really help me
very much.

There is an apparent contradiction at the end of the
gospels, when Jesus is saying farewell to his disciples. He
tells them to go off in all directions to make disciples of all
nations, and then adds: 'I will be with you always' (Matt.
28: 20). The explanation of this is to be found in the account
of Jesus's final teaching of his disciples before his death.
John records that Jesus said: 'I tell you the truth, it is for
your good that I am going away. Unless I go away, the
Counsellor will not come to you; but if I go, I will send him
to you' (John 16: 7), and here is the real answer to our
pilgrimage problem. The advantage of Jesus going away is
clear. The eternal and pre-existent Christ, through whom
the world was made, became a human being, without
ceasing to be God, but accepted the spatial limitations of
a human body. He is never recorded as having been out
fishing with Peter on the lake and at the same time climbing
a mountain with John. Now, he is telling the eleven apostles
to scatter to the ends of the earth. How can he possibly go
with all of them at once and keep his promise to be with

each one of them always? And so we realise that it is indeed to our advantage that he should go away, return to heaven and then send the Helper, the Holy Spirit, who can go with all of us wherever we go and also with anyone to whom we may speak at any time. It is the work of the Holy Spirit to make Jesus real and relevant to any of us at any time wherever we go.

The reason that many people cannot make sense of Christianity is a very simple one: they have never included the Holy Spirit in their explanations. We cannot understand how Jesus can help us today. The Holy Spirit relates the historical Jesus to the Jesus of experience, 'He will bring glory to me by taking from what is mine and making it known to you' (John 16: 14). We are all familiar with the possibility of looking at people and listening to people who are thousands of miles away from us and who, indeed, we may never meet in the flesh. The other day, I saw and listened to a man that I haven't seen since we were students together – on television. God has provided a kind of divine communication system for, as it were, immediate world-wide hook-up through the person of the Holy Spirit. Leave out the Holy Spirit and it is difficult to explain Christian belief satisfactorily. Once understand what he does, and it makes sense.

But surely, you say, that means believing in the Trinity, doesn't it?

We naturally find the mathematics of one equals three and three equals one somewhat confusing, and it certainly is if you try to understand it that way. Even on a Sunday-school level, however, we notice how in very cold weather our moist breath freezes into solid ice on the inside of the windscreen of our cars until the car heater has warmed up sufficiently to melt it into water which runs down to the bottom of the windscreen. We know that water vapour, liquid water and ice, although each quite distinct from the others, are all forms of the same substance with the molecular structure H_2O.

One of the most helpful analogies I have ever come across was in the detective writer Dorothy Sayers' book called *The Mind of the Maker*.[1] She suggests that a book like *Das Kapital*, for example, may be regarded as a trinity. First, there is the essential idea in the mind of Karl Marx: nobody else knows these ideas yet, apart perhaps from friends with whom he might share some of his ideas. *Das Kapital* thus exists as concept. But then the book is published and you can hold a volume in your hand and say, 'This is *Das Kapital*'. Now you have a manifestation or a concretisation of the concept which continues to exist in the author's mind. Thus, you now have two *Kapital*s distinct from each other, but both of them may be described as being *Das Kapital*.

Finally, people read the book, grasp the concept and seek to put it into practice. Now the third *Kapital*, this time in action. The concept still exists, the book still exists, but now the concept manifested in the book finds realisation. Notice that all three have to exist: any two would be insufficient by themselves. You must have a trinity.

In Christian thinking, God is the creator, unknown except to the Israelites; Jesus Christ the incarnate Word, who can be heard and touched, and then the Holy Spirit is God in action in the world, bringing into existence the new community. It is not three separate Gods any more than it is three separate *Kapital*s: in both cases there is only one entity, but each one of the three is related to and essential to the other two.

In Islam there is a great stress that Allah is One. Both the Old and New Testaments insist also on the Oneness of God (See Deut. 6: 4 and I Tim. 2: 5). But the Koran also speaks of God's Word and God's Spirit. But as God is eternal so also is his Word and his Spirit, so that even in Islam it is possible to think of a trinity not so dissimilar from that of the Bible.

The father and son analogy is a very helpful one in Asia, where a son authorised by his father would feel bound to do

all that his father commanded him, but unable to go beyond
the limits which have been set for him. If the son were
representing the father in a business matter, then anything
which you settled with the son would be regarded also as
settled with the father.

The following passage from the Bible shows all three
members of the Godhead interacting:

> You, however, are controlled not by the sinful nature
> but by the Spirit, if the *Spirit of God* lives in you. And
> if anyone does not have the *Spirit of Christ*, he does
> not belong to Christ. But if *Christ* is in you, your body
> is dead because of sin, yet your spirit is alive because
> of righteousness. And if the *Spirit of him who raised
> Jesus from the dead* is living in you, he who raised Christ
> from the dead will also give life to your mortal bodies
> through *his Spirit*, who lives in you (Rom. 8: 9–11, my
> italics).

HOW WOULD YOU
DEFINE A CHRISTIAN?

The simple anagram of the word Christian, moving the 'a'
to the beginning, produces: A Christ-In. A Christian is
somebody who has Christ in them. As expressed in the
song, which you may have heard, 'Lord of the Dance', 'I'll
live in you, if you'll live in me'.

But, how is it possible for Christ to live in somebody?
Through his Spirit.

In the quotation from Romans 8 above, 'If anyone does
not have the Spirit of Christ, he does not belong to Christ'
means, conversely, that if he does possess the Spirit of
Christ, then he does belong to him. Thus, Christians are
those who possess the Spirit of Christ dwelling within them.
Note that in these verses, he is called not only 'the Spirit of
Christ' and 'the Spirit of God' but also simply 'Christ . . . in

you' and again 'the Spirit of him who raised Jesus from the
dead' and finally, 'his Spirit'. That is, if one is indwelt by
one member of the Trinity, one is indwelt by all three. This
is implied by the promise of Jesus, 'My Father will love
him, and *we will come to him* and make *our* home with him'
(John 14: 23). In other words, becoming a Christian may be
described as inviting a takeover by God.

This concept at first sight may seem a frightening one.
Not only does it have something of a spooky feeling, but the
idea of being taken over by a power greater than ourselves is
perhaps alarming. C. S. Lewis has a nice illustration which
helps here. Dealing with the problem that we might face,
that if everyone of us is taken over by Christ, there might be
a monotonous sameness about us all, he uses the analogy of
salt. One could imagine that if one adds salt to a variety
of different kinds of food, every one of them would then
taste of nothing but salt. However, we all know that one of
the best ways to bring out the distinctive flavours of different
sorts of food is to add the right quantity of salt. Handing
ourselves over to God does not, in the event, blot out our
own personalities but, rather, enhances and enriches them.

In becoming a Christian we come under 'new ownership',
but we are still left as the local manager, with responsibility
for running the business and making the local decisions, in
accordance with the policy laid down by the new owner.
The picture of a small business owner who has become
totally bankrupt and who invites takeover by a new firm
with vast resources is, perhaps, a helpful one. But you may
prefer a poetic expression:

> Lord, my heart is a ghetto
> walled off
> dark
> depressed
> danger filled
> hurting.
> Move in, Lord.

Renew it
renew my heart
destroy, burn
raze
remove.
Build it fresh
and then You live there.
You Lord.
Because then
it'll stay
clean
pure
new.[2]

But how does a person become a Christian in the first place?

John's gospel describes a conversation one night between Jesus and the Pharisee leader, Nicodemus. Nicodemus starts off very politely, but Jesus knows that the aging Nicodemus is interested in the possibility of a fresh start.

In reply Jesus declared, 'I tell you the truth, unless a man is born again, he cannot see the kingdom of God.' 'How can a man be born when he is old?' Nicodemus asked. 'Surely he cannot enter a second time into his mother's womb to be born!' (John 3: 3–4).

A new birth is needed: not a repeat of physical birth by going back into his mother's womb, but a spiritual rebirth through the Spirit.

The parallel between natural birth and spiritual rebirth is an instructive one. One of those vivid human experiences, which I will never forget, is watching my children being born. It is a fantastic, ecstatic, almost miraculous experience. The small body emerges from his mother: it looks blue and you wonder whether it will ever live. And then, suddenly, a gasping breath and the baby goes bright red

and it's almost as though someone has pressed the button
and it's all systems go! Just as in natural birth, breath
enters the baby's body, so in supernatural birth, the breath
(Spirit) of God enters our hearts and souls. It is this crucial
entry of breath that brings a baby to independent human
life. In the same way, it is receiving the Spirit of Christ
into our lives which is the beginning of eternal life. Since
you started reading this chapter, you have been breathing
steadily but quite unconsciously and you have never needed
to remind yourself that you must at all costs go on breathing.
The 'takeover' by breath is in no way a frightening one and
one to which we are totally accustomed. In the same way, a
Christian who has been taken over by God's Spirit is only
aware of the indwelling Spirit when he deliberately chooses
to remind himself of the fact.

When a baby is born, it becomes a member of a human
family. In the same way, spiritual rebirth causes us to be
born again into the family of God. Thus, if we want to be
real Christians, then we must be born again, that is to say
we must receive Christ into our lives through his Spirit.

It is not really a question of there being a variety of
possible definitions of what a Christian is. We must surely
accept Christ's own definition of what is involved in becoming a Christian. The Christian Church has always had the
problem of well-meaning people who have merely imitated
Christians: who do all the things that Christians do, like
going to church services, reciting the Creed and seeking to
lead a moral life – but without this transforming experience
of receiving Christ through his Spirit, of experiencing this
takeover. I even have a clergyman friend in North Wales,
who is an ordained minister, conducting services and
preaching sermons and who was soundly converted one day
in the course of one of his own sermons, when he realised
that it really was all true!

I am not saying that there is any single, stereotyped
manner in which a person may be converted for, as Jesus
said to Nicodemus, 'The wind blows wherever it pleases.

You hear its sound, but you cannot tell where it comes from or where it is going. So it is with everyone born of the Spirit' (John 3: 8). It is none the less true that whether one is a Protestant or a Catholic, an Anglican or a Methodist, the only thing which makes a person clearly and definitely a Christian in this Biblical sense is receiving Christ through his Holy Spirit.

We should also notice that the new birth is directly related to faith in Jesus and his death on the cross. Nicodemus asks, 'How can this be?' (John 3: 9). Jesus replies by making reference to an occasion in Israel's history when the disobedient Israelites in the desert were afflicted by a plague of venomous snakes and many of them had been bitten and were dying (Num. 21: 9). Moses was instructed to make a model serpent out of bronze and to put it up on a pole. God then told him to tell the people that whoever looked at the serpent lifted up on the pole would live. The people are dying, their lives are over, but if only they will believe what God says and look at the model of the snake, then they will be born again and enjoy a new start. So Jesus says, 'Just as Moses lifted up the snake in the desert, so the Son of Man must be lifted up, that everyone who believes may in him have eternal life' (John 3: 14). It is not that there is any particular therapeutic value in brass, the people are saved from death because they believe what God tells them. In the same way, Jesus goes on to say, 'For God so loved the world that he gave his one and only Son, that whoever believes in him shall not perish, but have eternal life' (John 3: 16). In other words, they will be born again as a result of the cross of Jesus. Just as the brass serpent was a representation of the venomous, death-dealing vipers, so the cross of Jesus, dying under God's curse, reminds us of that deadly bite of sin which is bringing us to death.

How, then, is one born again? By believing in what God has said about his Son and by trusting in the Lord Jesus, who was lifted up to die for us, so that we might live and not perish. Thus, we see that the new birth from the Spirit of

Christ coming into us relates also to trusting in the Lord
Jesus who died for us on the cross.

But there is much more to this relationship than causing
us to be born again as real Christians or making Jesus real
to us. As we open our hearts to Christ and let him indwell
us by his Spirit, he also works in us to make us holy and to
make us like himself.

'Because through Christ Jesus the law of the Spirit of
Life set me free from the law of sin and death' (Rom. 8: 2).
You can understand this verse by imagining that you are
a person who has been infected with a fatal disease, the
body's defence system has been swamped and you, the
patient, are dying. You hurry to the doctor and ask him to
save you. He fills the syringe with an antibiotic and injects
this new principle into you which fights against the disease
and destroys it.

The verse above reminds us that sin, the inward moral
disease of the heart, is destroying us. We cry to Christ
for help: 'Please save me!' and he puts into us the new
principle of life through the Spirit, to overcome the power of
sin in us. Just as a battle goes on between the antibiotic and
the disease-causing bacteria, so a struggle goes on between
the Holy Spirit and sin as he systematically overcomes the
moral disease in our hearts.

It is not that we experience instant perfection the
moment we become Christians, any more than a patient is
immediately restored to blooming health the very moment
when the doctor injects him. It is much more of a progres-
sive convalescence, as the disease is eradicated and the
damage which it has done is gradually repaired. You are
saved the moment you are in the doctor's hands, but you
are not yet totally recovered. The seventeenth-century
writer from Kidderminster, Richard Baxter, once said that
'the church is a mere hospital'.

Christians are not, therefore, people who feel themselves
to be better than other people. Quite the reverse. They are
people who, recognising their sickness and their need of

treatment, have run to Christ and asked him to save them. Are you sensible to take offence when Christians who have become 'in-patients' in Christ's hospital call encouragingly through the windows saying, 'Come and try this doctor! We have found that he has the answer to our moral diseases. We're not totally recovered yet, but we are glad that we have put ourselves into his hands to treat us and we urge you to do the same.'

Continuing the injection analogy, vaccines are often prepared by taking serum from an animal which has deliberately been infected by disease and has overcome it and then giving these victorious antibodies to the victim, in order that that same victory might be repeated. The Spirit whom we receive in becoming a Christian is the Spirit of Christ who lived a perfect human life, victorious over all temptation, and who has decisively defeated sin on the cross. We are asking him, who has overcome sin himself, now through his Spirit to overcome sin in us.

What I have been describing in these recent paragraphs is what is technically called sanctification: the process by which Christians, by trusting in Jesus, become increasingly conformed to that pattern of perfect human life which he has set before us.

Notice here, incidentally, the contrast between the Christian religion and many other religions which see salvation as an ultimate goal which may be attained provided a sufficiently meritorious life has been achieved. Such religions provide a set of external rules which, if observed, guarantee salvation. By contrast, the Christian life offers salvation to start with: the moment we have put ourselves into the doctor's hands we are safe! The transformed life is the consequence of having been saved by Jesus, not the ground upon which salvation may be ultimately achieved. It is not that we become Christians by adherence to an external set of ethical rules, but rather that we are progressively transformed by the indwelling Holy Spirit of Christ, to become like Jesus.

Thus, being a Christian is not a question of 'Live a good life and then you will be saved,' but rather reverses this and says, 'First be saved and then the Saviour will enable you to lead a new life through his indwelling Spirit.'

Not only does the Holy Spirit work in individuals, one by one, but also in the Christian community as a whole. We have seen that we are born again not as isolated orphans but as members of the Christian family. It is, in fact, the Holy Spirit who links Christians together and builds them together into a 'dwelling in which God lives by his Spirit' (Eph. 2: 21–22). Many of the references to people being changed are plural rather than singular as, for example, 'We all . . . are being changed' from one degree of glory to another by 'the Lord who is the Spirit' (2 Cor. 3: 18, RSV). Thus, it is the work of the Holy Spirit to transform the imperfect community made up of unholy individuals, into a beautiful church community without spot or blemish (Eph. 5: 27). Being a Christian, then, is not an individualistic experience, but one which relates us to other people within God's family. Or, to pick up the earlier analogy, we become 'in-patients' together in Christ's hospital.

Finally, then, let me sum up the purpose of the Holy Spirit when he takes us over and lives in us.

* He makes us into real Christians by indwelling us, and causes us to be born again.
* He makes Jesus subjectively real to us, so that we experience Christ through his Spirit in our hearts.
* He works in us to transform us, both individually and corporately, to be more Christ-like.

I would like to use one final illustration, however. It may be that many of us hesitate to become Christians for fear that we might fail. We don't want to be wishy-washy, feeble, uncommitted Christians. Nor do we want to give up half way. How can we be certain that, having put our trust in Christ, we shall continue to live faithfully as Christians? May there not be all manner of irresistible temptations?

I remember the very first time that my wife and I returned from Japan, by ship, to Britain. We had been on board for five weeks and now, one cold, blustery January morning, through the sleet and murk, we could dimly make out the windswept coast of Torbay. There had been times when we had wondered whether we would ever see our native land again. And even now, was it possible that even in the next few hours we might meet some fatal disaster and perish? And then pocketa-pocketa, pocketa-pocketa, pocketa-pocketa . . . a little boat came chugging out from Brixham and struggled alongside the liner, swinging up and down in the waves. The pilot leaped from the deck of the tug on to a rope ladder and came on board, expressly in order to see that we would arrive safely at Tilbury Docks, avoiding wrecks, rocks, the Goodwin Sands and many other hazards we did not even notice. In the same way, God has given us his Holy Spirit to indwell us, to see that our salvation is safely completed and to guide us safely to our destination. Thus, we pray to a Father in heaven, and our Saviour is interceding for us in heaven, although we cannot see him now, but the Holy Spirit has been sent down to be right alongside us on earth, in order to ensure that we will arrive safely at our heavenly destination.

Chapter 7

THE RADICAL RETHINK

What steps are required of people who want to become followers of Jesus Christ today? No different from what they always have been: first we must repent and then we must believe. But both these words are commonly misunderstood and must therefore be explained. This chapter explains 'repentance' and the next 'faith'.

Repentance means a radical rethink of our lives. The stirring sermons preached by the apostles in the book of Acts always reach the point when they urge men to respond to God. When the Jews in Jerusalem are 'cut to the heart' and ask, 'Brothers, what shall we do?' Peter replies '*Repent* and be baptised, every one of you, in the name of Jesus Christ so that your sins may be forgiven. And you will receive the gift of the Holy Spirit.' And 'With many other words he warned them; and he pleaded with them, "Save yourselves from this corrupt generation"' (Acts 2: 37–40, my italics).

When Paul is speaking to Greeks in Athens he says, 'In the past God overlooked such ignorance, but now he commands all people everywhere to *repent*' (Acts 17: 30, my italics).

Both John the Baptist and Jesus himself had gone around Palestine commanding men to *repent*, and it is clear that the activity of the apostles was following both the precedent and the command given by Jesus himself so that, just before returning to heaven, Jesus declared, 'This is what is written: The Christ will suffer and rise from the dead on the third day, and *repentance* and forgiveness of sins will be preached in his name to all nations' (Luke 24: 46–47, my italics).

What then did they mean by repentance?

The idea of repentance to many people just means being sorry for doing something wrong and is identified, also wrongly, with ideas like penitence and even penance. But, as we shall see, what the New Testament suggests is a thoroughgoing and radical reorientation of the whole life. The original word, *metanoia*, means to change your mind. We are used to the word *meta-morphosis*, meaning the kind of radical change of form that occurs between a caterpillar and a chrysalis and the butterfly, and *para-noia* meaning being alongside your mind, but also implying a thoroughgoing personality change. *Metanoia*, repentance, therefore, while it includes being sorry, confessing sin and apologising for it, means also a radical rethinking of attitudes and reorientation of lifestyle.

Becoming a Christian is not just a matter of adding a few religious beliefs to our memory bank, or even deciding that to become a Christian might be quite a good thing. It involves an entirely new allegiance which revolutionises everything. Some parallels might be a rebel changing sides, giving his allegiance to his king, the outlaw who becomes a sheriff, the politician who crosses the floor of the House to join the opposing party, or somebody returning to the life partner they had abandoned.

A very closely associated idea to that of 'repenting' is that of 'turning'. The two words are often found together, as for example when Paul is describing his commission from God:

> I am sending you to open their eyes and *turn them from* darkness to light, and from the power of Satan to God, so that they may receive forgiveness of sins and a place among those who are sanctified by faith in me . . . I preached that they should *repent* and *turn to God* and prove their repentance by deeds (Acts 26: 17–20, my italics).

It is much more than feeling sorry for having sinned, or feeling embarrassed at having been found out, despairing at losing one's self-respect because of moral failure or ashamed at losing face before others. Certainly, all of these subjective feelings may accompany repentance, just as on the Day of Pentecost the people were 'deeply troubled' or 'cut to the heart'. They were already feeling like this when they were told to repent.

Repentance is, then, much more than feelings and involves action to change and turn. In this sense, conversion is something which man is called upon to do: repent, turn and convert! Notice, incidentally, how different this idea is from the Buddhist concept of waiting passively for an experience of enlightenment. Christian conversion takes place when man obeys God's command to repent.

THE SERMON ON THE MOUNT: REPENTANCE

Let me try to list some of the factors involved in repentance, drawing from Jesus' Sermon on the Mount.

Repentance means recognising that I am spiritually destitute

In the Sermon on the Mount Jesus says, 'Blessed are the poor in spirit, for theirs is the kingdom of heaven' (Matt. 5: 3). Congratulations to those who are poor in spirit!

The Greeks had another word for poverty which meant unfortunates who had no property of their own and so had to work for a living, so that it described people who were not rich, landed gentry! However, the word Jesus uses (*ptochoi*) means people who are totally destitute, who have no property, no place, no job, no source of income, nothing to eat and, indeed, are up to their ears in debt so that, should they be given money, they would immediately lose it to their creditors. When we use the term poor in English, we are often only describing people who are not particularly well off and, indeed, whose pride is proverbial in their refusal to accept handouts and charity of any kind. But the people who are as destitute as this have no room for any pride at all, they can only beg. The only way to get out of such bankruptcy is the unmerited help of others. They are the paupers, the widows, the cripples. The same word is used of the Laodicean Christians when they are being urged to repent and are told that they are 'wretched, pitiful, poor, blind and naked' (Rev. 3: 17).

In the parable of the Pharisee and the tax collector, the latter knows that he is morally bankrupt and spiritually destitute and can only pray, 'God have mercy on me, a sinner.' He is hopelessly in moral debt, for which he can make no restitution, and he is incapable of delivering himself. There is no one in the kingdom of Christ who is not destitute in spirit. Martin Luther said, 'We are all beggars.' In the filthy rags of our own religious righteousness, defiled by unclean motives, with contaminated and sin-stained minds and no resources to offer, we fall before the great King, begging for grace. This is the kind of attitude which David expressed in Psalm 51.

Repentance means mourning over my sin

'Blessed are those who mourn, for they will be comforted' (Matt 5: 4).

This mourning is not bereavement over the loss of loved ones, but grief over my own sinfulness and failure. Like Isaiah when he saw the holiness of God, we cry, 'Woe to me! I am ruined! For I am a man of unclean lips . . .' (Isa. 6: 5). It is not enough to recognise my poverty objectively: I *must* mourn over it and be grieved over it subjectively. When Peter heard the cock crow, reminding him that he had denied his Lord, he went out and wept bitterly.

There is a tremendous paradox here: happy are the unhappy. It is a blessed condition to be in, when we are no longer thick-skinned and hardened by sin, but distressed because of things we have done or said or people we've hurt and cannot unhurt. Even in sport we can feel mortified because we've dropped a catch at cricket or missed a shot at golf, but how much deeper ought that distress to be when we have failed to hit a moral target at which we have aimed. It is good, Jesus says, to be broken-hearted, for that is a necessary condition of being comforted.

But who is it who will comfort us? The Jews hesitated to use the name of God because it was so holy. Thus, they preferred to talk about 'the kingdom of heaven' or 'at the right hand of the Majesty on high' rather than use God's name. They also used what is called the reverential passive as here: 'They shall be comforted', in the same way in which in some Asian languages you can use an honorific and say, 'They shall be honourably comforted'; and everybody knows at once whom you mean. It is God himself who comforts those who mourn over their sins.

We know that this idea was very much to the forefront of Jesus's mind at the beginning of his ministry, because when he first taught in the synagogue at Nazareth, he read the words, 'The Lord has anointed me to preach good news to the poor . . . He has sent me to *comfort all who mourn*, and provide for those who grieve in Zion to bestow on them a crown of beauty instead of ashes, the oil of gladness instead of mourning' (Isa. 61: 1–3, my italics). Jesus, then, will give joy to the person who mourns, and who is genuinely sorry for their sins. Repentance is not just shame or sorrow: broken-heartedness is the way to blessedness.

Repentance results in mercy to others
'Blessed are the merciful, for they will be shown mercy' (Matt. 5: 7).

The servant who has been forgiven a huge debt by the king, in the parable of the unforgiving servant (Matt. 18: 23–35) should have extended the same forgiveness to those who owed him a relatively small amount. The unmerited grace which I have had from God in forgiving my sins must then be extended by me to those who have sinned against me. Up till now, I may have been cynical, bitter and resentful. All that kind of thing must be changed. I must extend the same mercy to others that I have already received myself. This is quite the reverse of a Pharisaical and judging attitude towards others. A Christian is not somebody who regards himself as very holy and, therefore, censorious of others. He is, rather, somebody who knows that he is an undeserving sinner who has received mercy and therefore longs to share that mercy with others.

Repentance means reconciliation and restitution
'Blessed are the peacemakers, for they will be called sons of God' (Matt. 5: 9).

   This involves making restitution to other people if our sin has affected them. It means returning what we have stolen, apologising when we have hurt people, being reconciled where there has been estrangement, putting right anything that has been wrong.

   When Zacchaeus repented he gave back to people with interest what he had wrongfully taken from them. There will be books on our shelves which we have failed to return, or debts which we have conveniently forgotten to repay. The result of being reconciled to God is that we take steps to be reconciled to men.

Repentance means hungering to live differently
'Blessed are those who hunger and thirst for righteousness, for they will be filled' (Matt. 5: 6).

   Repentance means rejecting and abandoning every known sin in our lives, where our consciences have been accusing us and where we have been disobeying God's commandments. It means positively seeking to obey God in doing what is good, as well as in abandoning what is evil. A moral standard that involves 'never doing anybody any harm' is clearly inadequate when compared with one which demands that we always do everybody as much good as we possibly can.

This point can be illustrated in various ways. Mathematicians may prefer a graph in which the area below the zero line may be described as vice and that above it as virtue. Repentance demands much more than merely not being vicious but asks, rather, that we should be enthusiastically virtuous. Repentance, then, means not only abandoning vice but embracing virtue.

Or, if one prefers a more homely metaphor, found in the New Testament, we are to 'put off' certain vices and to 'put on' other virtues. J. B. Phillips' translation of Ephesians 5 is most striking: 'What you learned was to fling off the dirty clothes of the old ways of living, which were rotted through and through with lust's illusions, and, with yourselves mentally and spiritually remade, to put on the clean fresh clothes of the new life.' It is not enough merely to take off all the stinking, filthy, dirty old clothes. When we have got rid of all of our vices, we are still stark naked. Rather, having had a complete bath (for Christ has washed our hearts and consciences clean), there is that marvellous feeling of those crisp, new, clean clothes freshly ironed and warmed from the heavenly airing cupboard! This, then, is a vivid biblical description of what repentance involves.

John the Baptist urged those who repent to 'Produce fruit in keeping with repentance' (Matt. 3: 8). Do you really want to be different? This whole concept of repentance really begins to bite; you may not really want to live differently at all. You are more likely to be asking questions like, will I have to give up getting drunk or going to bed with my girlfriend/boyfriend? There is often a funny contradiction here, for it is possible to be quite critical of other people who call themselves Christians but whose lives are not consistent. Do we really want to become Christians who are wishy-washy and half-hearted, or are we going to be determined to obey all the commandments of Christ whatever the consequences? I have no authority to water down the ethical demands of becoming a Christian: nobody has. I have already sought to make the point that Christian ethics are not merely a matter of not smoking, for example (so that a Christian is chiefly distinguished by the enjoyable things which he does not do!), but rather that our lives should be positively full of beautiful characteristics, namely, that righteousness which it is good to hunger and thirst after.

It is worth making the point here that Christians flee from fornication and adultery because they are commanded to do so by Christ. It is not that Christians have a low view of sex or think that sex is intrinsically dirty. On the contrary, it is because Christians have a very high view of sex and what a good thing it is, that they refuse to fool around with it or to treat it as a physiological toy. It is certainly not that Christians have a 'kill joy' attitude towards sex, but rather that they have a 'keep joy' attitude towards it. Sex is such a wonderfully good and enjoyable thing to enrich and deepen the relationship between two people who are committed to each other within a secure marriage relationship. This is quite different from surreptitious and clandestine physiological explorations which may even be exploitation of another person, to whom we are not committed and have no intention of ever being committed. We would also question whether hurrying from one broken relationship into another, in order to fill the vacuum created by the break, is ultimately going to help a person to build a stable, committed relationship.

The same thing can be illustrated from drunkenness. Wine, like sex, is a gift of God when properly used. To finish up out of control, behaving wildly and irresponsibly, a comic nuisance to other people, vomiting on the stairs and finishing in a state of coma, is a misuse of what the Psalmist calls 'wine that gladdens the heart of man' (Ps. 104: 15), or as an enjoyable drink for the wedding guests in Cana or at the solemnity of the Last Supper, when Jesus spoke of the fruit of the vine. Christians, then, should have no hangups over sex and drink as such, but only over their misuse. In any case, as we have seen, it is a mistake to concentrate on

things that Christians do not do when we ought to be
thinking much more positively.

Repentance means public alignment with the cause of Christ

'Blessed are those who are persecuted because of righteousness, for theirs is the kingdom of heaven. Blessed are you
when people insult you and falsely say all kinds of evil
against you because of me. Rejoice and be glad, because
great is your reward in heaven, in the same way they
persecuted the prophets who were before you' (Matt. 5:
10–12).

We have to face the fact that people may be hostile to
Christ's kingdom. Even though King Herod was eighty at
the time, he felt threatened by the infant Jesus when the
Wise Men called him 'one born to be king of the Jews'.
Herod wiped out a whole row of children, in order to make
certain of killing anybody who might take his throne. Jesus
himself said, 'If they persecuted me they will persecute you
also' (John. 15: 20).

To be a Christian means identifying yourself with an
unpopular minority. You have to be willing to be known as
a Christian and to associate with other Christians.

Christians were persecuted from the earliest days of the
Acts of the Apostles. There were terrible persecutions under
the Roman Empire. In Cambridge, a group of students
studied the banned Greek New Testament in the White-
horse Inn, and some of them later died for their convictions;
there is the Martyrs' Memorial in Oxford, where later
Wesley and his friends were despised as 'Methodists'. That
persecution continues up to the present day.

I was talking the other day to two Nepalis. In their
country, one goes to prison for one year for being baptised
and for six years for baptising somebody else.

An Egyptian Muslim told his wife that he had become a
Christian. At first, she was fearful because of his foolhardi-
ness (under the Shariah, Muslim law, it is no crime to kill

somebody who defects from Islam), but as she had noted
and approved the transformation in his life, she agreed to
believe with him, but it was too dangerous for them either
to remain in their home or to move out, and they just
walked out with what they could carry.

A Malay who becomes a Christian might expect poison
in his food, and I know of Chinese young people who have
been beaten by their parents for believing in Christ.

By contrast, we seem a bit feeble if all the persecution we
are shrinking from is the laughter and mockery of a few
erstwhile friends (if they are real friends, it won't make any
difference to them, and if they are not real friends we are
not losing much anyway!). While in this more tolerant age
people who take their Christianity seriously meet less opposition than they used to, I have been quite surprised at the
extent to which Christians in some tertiary institutions are
much spoken against as a despised minority. Jesus made it
perfectly clear that if we become Christians we must be
ready to identify ourselves with him and with those who
follow him.

For others, a chief fear is the reaction of a girlfriend or
boyfriend, or prospective marriage partner. You may fear
they will reject you if you become a real Christian and
accept Christian standards.

I remember on one mission, a man in fear and trembl-
ing finally decided to take the decisive step to become
a Christian. A very anxious letter postmarked Cambridge
then went across to Oxford and crossed in the post with
another rather scared letter addressed to Cambridge and
postmarked Oxford. His fiancée had become a Christian
the same week, quite independently. Unfortunately, I
cannot guarantee that this will always happen! It may be
weeks or months before the other person shares your convictions, or perhaps the friendship will be broken. There is
nothing new in this – such problems are described in the
New Testament.

Repentance, then, is a whole reorientation of personality,

a radical transformation of thought, attitude, outlook and direction. How radical it is is illustrated by the use of 'turn' and 'return' in the Old Testament. Isaiah calls, 'Return to him you have so greatly revolted against' (Isa. 31: 6). While the Lord says, 'Return to me . . . and I will return to you' (Zech. 1: 3; *cf.* Mal. 3: 7). It is used for a faithless wife returning to her husband. 'I will go back to my husband as at first' (Hos. 2: 7). There clearly would be grief and sorrow at the extent of the previous failure but, also, tremendous joy at the restoration of a relationship that had been broken. Moreover, the returning would mean a total realignment of loyalty and a fresh outpouring of love and service.

It is also used for a rebel laying down his arms and coming back to serve his rightful king. God commands repentance. We ought not to think that we are doing God some kind of favour in becoming a Christian. Nor are we doing so merely because it is to our selfish advantage to do so. We are to respond this way because it is the only right way to respond, as wilful and treacherous rebels who have behaved so shamefully in fighting against a just and long-suffering king.

This reminds us how foolish is the view that we can wait until the last moment for a death-bed repentance. Not to repent is an offence to God, who commands repentance *now*. What is the point of repenting when you have no time left to serve the King? Our sincerity is in doubt if we postpone repentance. Moreover, hesitation implies doubt of God's good faith. He is urging us to return and is declaring his welcome, but this sense of misgiving on our part is perfectly understandable and normal. We do find it very difficult to believe that, when we have badly fouled things up and hurt and wounded somebody else, we really could be welcomed back. The story of the Prodigal Son tells us how the father is watching for his son's return and when he is on his way back, his father sees him while still a great way off and runs and, indeed, in the words of the Authorized Version, 'fell on his neck and kissed him'. Can God really be as good as that?

Human relationships give some feeble shadow of the joys of reconciliation.

The story is told of a young man in Japan who, having greatly shamed his family by falling into disgrace, writes and asks that if he really is welcome home they would put a small hand-towel in the window where he may see it from the passing train and thus know that he is welcome back. If it's not there, then he will just remain on the train and not alight at the station. As the train comes round the bend, he anxiously looks out of the train window to see if the towel is there or not, only to discover that there are towels in every window, hanging on the washing-line and even from the fruit trees. There is absolutely no doubt of his welcome back, and we can imagine his delight as he leaps down from the train and runs home to his family. There is no doubt that, in the Bible as a whole, God declares unashamedly his love for us in spite of all our failures, and that he calls us to return to him.

THE RESULTS OF REPENTANCE

1. Forgiveness of sins

Passage after passage in the New Testament makes forgiveness conditional upon repentance (e.g. Luke 24: 47; Acts 3: 19, 5: 31, 26: 18). I must repent if I want to be forgiven. The ground of forgiveness is not my repentance but the death of Christ, because Christ died for me that I might be forgiven. But my repentance is my turning towards God that makes the death of Christ available and effective for me. It is not my hand or the switch which provides the power, but the dynamos in the power station. But when the switches are thrown across from one direction to the other, that instant the power begins to flow, and so Peter tells the man at the Beautiful Gate, 'Repent, then, and turn to God, so that your sins may be wiped out . . .' (Acts 3: 19). As my attitudes switch across, so I experience the forgiveness of sins.

Sometimes we may be thoroughly miserable over our guilt
and sense of uncleanness and of defilement. We all know the
wonder of the feeling when we are dirty, grimy, of having a
really good bath, feeling really clean again. It is repentance,
then, that brings us to Jesus for him to cleanse us and make
us clean again.

2. Joy in heaven

'There is more rejoicing in heaven over one sinner who
repents than over ninety-nine righteous persons who do not
need to repent' (Luke 15: 7).

It is really astonishing to think that heaven should be so
interested in what I do, and that my response should cause
such a positive reaction there. Both the shepherd and the
woman in the parables called in their neighbours to share
their rejoicing. When Matthew was called to follow Jesus,
he immediately threw a party, so that his friends could meet
his new Master. When Zacchaeus was converted, he also
threw a repentance party, to declare his new allegiance and
pin his colours to the mast. It is not uncommon, when a
person is converted, that their non-Christian friends feel in
some way cut off from them and, perhaps, there would be
no better way of showing continuing desire for friendship
than to throw a party to celebrate them having become
Christians. We should notice that whereas repentance is
often identified with a feeling of penitence, sackcloth and
ashes, the Christian emphasis is that true repentance brings
rejoicing, not only among the angels in heaven, but among
our friends on earth.

But, will we repent and change our minds? John declares
God's readiness to accept us if we do. 'If we confess our sins,
he is faithful and just and will forgive us our sins and purify
us from all unrighteousness' (1 John 1: 9). May I suggest
you spend some time now deciding whether or not you are
willing to confess your sins, not to men, but to God. Are you
ready to open your heart and pour it out before him, and to
repent of your sins and to confess them to him? If you do, he

promises both to forgive you and to cleanse you, and what rejoicing that will bring.

This is the way one modern writer has expressed it. It is really a prayer:

> Many times I've been smiling
> When inside I've been crying,
> I've been shaking hands with people
> Who just didn't know my pain.
>
> Many times I've been walking
> When inside I've been running,
> I've been standing in the sunshine
> But could only feel the rain.
>
> Many times I've been winning
> When inside I was losing –
> Well, I liked to hear the cheering
> But it didn't ease my mind.
>
> Lord, I'm weary
> That is why my head is bowed,
> And I've had my share of running
> Running with the crowd.
>
> I've had my share of reaching out
> But never really touching,
> Lord, let me feel the healing touch
> Of Jesus in my soul.
>
> I've had my share of crying out
> But never really praying –
> Lord, I want to say I'm sorry, will you
> Come and make me whole.[1]

Chapter 8

FAITH – TRUSTING IN ANOTHER

There can be few people who do not know that being a Christian has something to do with faith. However, not many people could define clearly what they mean by this, and still fewer could explain exactly what Christians mean by it.

Emmerson said that faith is the rejection of a lesser fact and the acceptance of a greater; Christians say that God is that greater fact.

One modern Christian writer has said, 'Faith is our response to God's initiative . . . Great faith is responding to God when it is hardest to do so, either when the thing he demands of you hurts, or else it seems totally impractical.'

Is it a matter of willpower, then? Faith is rather to do with a personal relationship. This is faith in *someone*.

Jesus told a story which illustrates this beautifully:

> Two men went up to the temple to pray, one a Pharisee and the other a tax collector. The Pharisee stood up and prayed about himself: 'God, I thank you that I am not like all other men – robbers, evildoers, adulterers – or even like this tax collector. I fast twice a week and give a tenth of all I get.' But the tax collector stood at a distance. He would not even look up to heaven, but beat his breast and said, 'God, have mercy on me, a sinner.' I tell you that this man, rather than the other, went home justified before God. For everyone who exalts himself will be humbled, and he who humbles himself will be exalted (Luke 18: 10–14).

WHO IS TRUSTING WHOM
IN THIS STORY?

Modern-day readers have their own problems in under-standing this story of Jesus, because they tend to think of the Pharisees as hypocritical 'baddies' whereas there is no doubt that, in their own day, they were widely respected as being 'goodies'. They were the most committed group of dedicated Jews, who took their religion extremely seriously, determined to keep their traditional Jewish religious values pure in spite of dangerous foreign influence, and scrupulous in seeking to obey all six hundred and thirteen com-mandments found in the Jewish Law. The Pharisee is speaking the absolute truth when he describes himself as a man of real integrity in matters of money, morals and sex, scrupulously self-disciplined ('I fast twice a week') and whose faith touched his pocket ('I give a tenth of all I get').

The tax collector worked for the Roman occupying power – having sold his soul for money, betraying his national loyalty to work for the enemy because it was a lucrative way of earning a living. He was undeniably a baddie in the eyes of any decent patriotic Jew.

The Bible says that the tax collector 'went home justified before God'. So does God justify a bad man, but reject a good man? The key is to ask very simply: Who is trusting in whom? The Pharisee's religion is reminiscent of what we sometimes rather rudely call 'public school religion' – if you lead a decent life and are a decent, nice person then God, who is also a nice, decent Person will accept you. Just listen to this man: 'I thank you that I am not . . . I fast . . . and give . . .' The Pharisee is trusting in his own good character, in his sincere good life and in his scrupulous religious observances. Clearly, he is not really trusting in God even though he prays to him, but is trusting *himself*.

Listen now to the other man: 'God have mercy on me, a

sinner.' Who is this man trusting in? He cannot trust in his own character – he knows he is a sinner. He cannot trust in his own worthy actions – he has sinned. He puts all his confidence therefore in the character and actions of God. God is a God whose character is merciful and who has mercy upon sinners.

Do you begin to see what Christians mean by *faith*? They mean trust in Somebody else: dependence upon God. A Christian is somebody who trusts in the holiness and righteousness of God and, particularly, in what God has done in Christ, reconciling the world to himself by his death on the cross. It is not trust in his own character or actions, but trust in the character and actions of God.

I could almost stop at this point and ask which of these two people you identify with? This is not so simple as it sounds. If you are straightforward, decent-living people, and most of us probably are in everyday terms, it is *humiliating* to admit that, in God's sight, we are sinners. We would prefer to try and get by on our own personal score, rather than to admit that the only way to be justified before God, is to ask him to do it. Are our decent character and moral efforts worth nothing? We just do not like having to admit that we are spiritually destitute and impoverished.

If we think about it, however, we will recognise that it is not any particular credit to us, personally, that we happen to have been born in a decent stable home which encouraged decent moral standards. Had we been born into a thoroughly disturbed and broken home we might well be very different sorts of people: mean, grasping and entirely self-centred by nature. And perhaps we still are, in spite of our advantages?

What we should notice, however, is that salvation by self-effort works rather unfairly. Some people are so pleasant by nature that they would attain almost without trying. Others would have such a burden of inherited evil temperament and environmental disadvantage that they would not have the slightest hope of salvation. By contrast, God has set his standards so high that all of us, however decent, are seen to be sinners. Some of us may feel ourselves to be moral giants compared with other depraved moral dwarfs. Viewed from the exalted summit of God's ethical Everest, however, we all seem dwarfed into moral insignificance.

A VICIOUS CIRCLE?

This is not the only difficulty which people have about faith, however. The one I have outlined above may not be your chief problem at all. You might express your problem like this: I can't believe in Christ unless I have faith, but I can't have faith unless I believe in Christ. Some Christians seem to be saying 'you must have faith to believe'. Then where do I get it from? How do I get it? Faith seems to be some nebulous quantity that I certainly do not possess. I cannot believe that my friends (and after all some of them weren't Christians a year ago) are just credulous idiots whose inadequate personalities mean that they have to trust in something. But how do they screw up faith to believe?

We are still thinking like the small boy whose definition was that 'Faith is believing something that isn't true.' It may help for a moment to review the three different ways in which the New Testament talks about 'believing'.

1. Faith involves believing facts
The tax collector believed in the existence of God and in the fact that God had been revealed to be merciful. We have already spent a good deal of time discussing the facts about Christ proclaimed by the apostles, believed by the first Christians and sung about in the early churches. You do not have to study theology in order to become a Christian any more than you have to study gastric enzymology before eating or psychology before thinking. It is accessible and understandable to the ordinary man and, indeed, even to

totally illiterate people. But there is a certain minimal content of essential facts that have to be believed. That God the Creator exists: that God has spoken through the prophets and, supremely, in Jesus Christ; and that Jesus Christ is Lord, the Son of God, that he died on the cross on our behalf and that God raised him from the dead. Faith must have a content of facts. I cannot just urge somebody who knows nothing about Jesus Christ to believe in him. Faith must have some objective content.

The man in a burning aeroplane who climbs into a rucksack, under the mistaken impression that it is a parachute, and jumps out of the aeroplane, will be disappointed before he reaches the ground. The facts must be examined first. You must satisfy yourself, as best you can, that it is indeed a parachute and not a rucksack that you have hold of. Merely to possess a parachute is, in itself, not enough and there is only one way to discover whether that particular parachute will work for you. But before you take such an irrevocable step of jumping out of the aeroplane, you must know a minimum amount about parachutes.

Having stressed the importance of believing facts, however, the following qualifications are also necessary.

(i) Knowledge of the facts does not provide absolute proof
You may know the story of the ten atheists who were determined to settle the existence of God one way or the other, once and for all. One of them took out his watch and asked that, if God were real, he would strike him dead in ten seconds. After nine seconds had passed, the man collapsed, fell over and died. The other nine were considerably shaken and, having satisfied themselves that he was dead, one of them advanced the solution that the man had been under such psychological stress and suspense that he had died of a heart attack and that it was pure coincidence. This man now, in turn, immediately collapsed and died. Whereupon the other eight all became convinced believers!

But what sort of a belief is that? Their decision to believe
was not made willingly from choice but because to do anything else would be foolish and fatal.[1] There must always be
just enough lack of demonstrative certainty to make a free
choice possible. If the proof of Christianity was as demon-
strable as geometry or arithmetic, we would have no option
but to believe, but it wouldn't be belief in a Christian sense.
It must be 'a convincing hypothesis' even if it falls short of
final proof with experimental confirmation. We can study
aerodynamics about parachutes, we can read accounts or
watch films of other people using parachutes, but there is no
absolute proof that this particular parachute will open for
me – and only one way to find out. C. S. Lewis is very
helpful on this subject:

> I do not think there is a *demonstrative* proof of Christi-
> anity, nor of the existence of matter, nor of the goodwill
> and honesty of my best and oldest friends. I think all
> three are (except perhaps the second) far more prob-
> able than the alternative . . . As to *why* God doesn't
> make it demonstrably clear: are we sure that He is even
> interested in the kind of theism which would be a
> compelled, logical assent to a conclusive argument?
> Are *we* interested in it, in personal matters? I demand
> from my friend a trust in my good faith which is *certain*
> without demonstrative proof. It wouldn't be confidence
> at all if you waited for rigorous proof.

(ii) Belief in facts alone is not enough

I believe in the existence of God: but so does the devil, and
it doesn't make him a believer. I can leap foolishly from the
aeroplane, shouting that I believe in parachutes, but that
won't help much either. Belief in the existence of doctors in
general, or the efficacy of some medicine in particular,
makes no difference by itself, unless we go to the doctor and
swallow his medicine.

*(iii) It is not faith which saves, but the person in whom you put your
faith*

A coupling will not pull a railway train, but a powerful
locomotive will. Faith is like the coupling that joins me to
the saving power of God.

2. Faith involves believing statements

'If you believed Moses, you would believe me; for he wrote
about me. But since you do not believe what he wrote, how
are you going to believe what I say?' (John 5: 46–47).

Faith is not only believing facts about Jesus but believing
the words which he says and acting upon them. We usually
believe the word that somebody speaks because we believe
them to be reliable people, so that this category leads very
naturally on to the third one.

3. Faith involves believing in a person

The word faith seems too abstract, whereas belief points to
a more active thought. In John's gospel we do not find the
word 'faith' at all, but no less than ninety-eight times we
do find the verb 'to believe'. This reminds us that faith in
Christ is something dynamic and not static. To trust in a
person is more than believing facts.

Believing in doctors is more than believing that doctors
exist, but means going to a particular doctor and putting
your life in his hands, drinking his medicine, obeying his
orders and even letting him put you to sleep and chop bits
out of you. That is much closer to what a Christian means
when he says that he believes in Jesus: he trusts him, he
depends upon him, he puts his life into the hands of Jesus.
Being a Christian then is an existential relationship with a
person you know, not merely believing in the existence of
somebody you have never met.

I hope that you are seeing this much more clearly now;
but some people do have problems because they think that
belief is screwing up enough of a quantity called faith and

hanging grimly on to that belief through thick and thin, without ever getting any further evidence than we had at the beginning. This is a terrible misunderstanding, as I must now try to explain.

Some people think that faith is like sitting down upon an imaginary chair so that if only your faith is strong enough, there really will be a chair there, brought into existence through the strength of your faith. Frankly, a man who sits down on something which isn't there is a fool and deserves to bump himself badly. That isn't faith at all, but only credulity. At the same time, faith is not merely believing that a certain object is a chair. This would be mere credence. You can look at the chair and examine it and decide that it probably would support your weight. But merely to believe in the existence of chairs, or that any particular chair might support your weight, is not faith in a biblical sense.

Faith means that you sit on it, and rest your weight upon it. In other words, after we have examined the probable hypothesis that Jesus is the Son of God, the Lord and Saviour of the world, we then believe in him and rest our weight in confidence and dependence upon him. This can all be illustrated from the story in John's gospel about the healing of the nobleman's son.

> There was a certain royal official whose son lay sick at Capernaum. When this man heard that Jesus had arrived in Galilee from Judea, he went to him and begged him to come and heal his son, who was close to death . . . The royal official said, 'Sir, come down before my child dies.' Jesus replied, 'You may go. Your son will live.' The man took Jesus at his word and departed. While he was still on the way, his servants met him with the news that his boy was living. When he enquired as to when his son got better, they said to him, 'The fever left him yesterday at the seventh hour.' Then the father realised that this was the exact time at

which Jesus had said to him, 'Your son will live.' So he
and all his household believed (John 4: 46–53).

It is an interesting question to ask ourselves when this
man first started believing in Jesus. On two occasions, he is
explicitly said to believe but in fact, a little thought reveals
that he must already have believed (in some sense) in order
to leave his dying child to come where Jesus was. We may,
in fact discover from this story three specific stages in the
development of faith.

(i) Potential Faith

When he went to Jesus, he already believed that Jesus could
do something for him, or he would not have left his dying
child. From what he has heard from others, it seems possible,
even probable, that Jesus can help him in his situation. But
though he has heard from others, he has never met Christ
before for himself.

This, frankly, is the situation of many well-meaning
religious people: the kind of people who go to church occasionally, but who feel that some people take religion too far,
very often have a real potential faith. Such a person really
does believe that Jesus *can* do things for him, and indeed
could do it for him *if* he ever needed Jesus to do so. It's just
that the situation has never arisen.

It is, thus, an authentic kind of faith but not satisfactory
unless it serves to lead you on to the subsequent stages.
There is a sense in which this kind of faith is equivalent to
believing in the *facts* about Jesus, which is obviously essential but not, by itself, adequate as a fully biblical faith. It
is possible to recite the Apostle's Creed in church and to
believe all the facts which it contains, but still only to be in
this position of potential faith.

(ii) Bare Faith

The Bible specifically says that the royal official 'took Jesus
at his word and departed'.

It never seems to have entered his head yet that Jesus can heal without visiting the sick child and with just the word 'your son will live'. The Bible just tells us that the man believed, but one wonders what went through his mind as he stood there in front of Jesus. It seemed that the interview was over. Should he argue? Or ask for more convincing proof? Or accept the word of Jesus? And the man believed without any means of checking up on it. If Jesus said it, then he would believe it.

Let us see then if we can come up with a satisfactory definition of this stage of faith: *faith is acting upon a convincing hypothesis which cannot be proved apart from personal experimental demonstration.*

There can be no absolute proof of some things without doing them: like knowing whether a parachute will work for you. A general belief in the efficacy of parachutes will only become experience if we put one on and jump. But will this particular parachute open? There is only one possible way of finding out.

It's a little like the Irishman who refused to get into the water until he had first learned to swim. It does seem, therefore, that a step or leap of faith is essential. The royal official believed what Jesus said and acted upon it. From the potential faith of believing that *Jesus can* he moves on to a bare faith of believing that *Jesus will*. Marriage involves a similar act of faith. We can think and consider and weigh up all the pros and cons but, ultimately, a decision and a commitment have to be made. You have examined and made certain that it is a parachute, and there is now a very high degree of probability that the parachute will open for you. You must therefore now trust the parachute and commit yourself to it and leap.

(iii) Confirmed Faith

The mistake that many people make is to imagine that they must for ever hang grimly on in faith with no more than intellectual probability and a total lack of evidence. But it is not like that at all! The royal official on his way home first meets the servants, who tell him that his son is better and that this recovery began yesterday, just at the time when Jesus spoke to him. Now, within twenty-four hours, he is no longer in the position of bare faith when he first accepted what Jesus said. In fact, he was just as secure then as he is now, but his faith is tremendously encouraged and helped by the evidence and the experience which confirm that he took the right step.

The man who sits in the chair – made of tungsten-reinforced steel and set in concrete – finds it will just about bear his weight! The man who jumps from the parachute soon knows if it has opened. The man who trusts the doctor begins to feel better. The person who gets married feels increasingly happily secure in the new relationship.

The person who becomes a Christian soon has evidence of the reality of God in his life. Before, he felt that God was his enemy, always forbidding and pursuing him: now, he knows that God is his friend. Before, he was more or less indifferent to sin and relatively unconcerned about it: now, he finds increasingly that he hates and loathes it. Formerly, he had little interest in the Bible, but now he knows that God speaks through it. He found himself somewhat impatient of Christians, even though some of them might be people he respected, they all seemed to be tiresome people trying to get him to meetings and to share their faith. Now, he regards them as his brothers. In all sorts of ways, he seeks God's help in answer to his prayers, and he finds that God does indeed answer them. Thus, bare faith is soon strengthened by experience to become an assured and confirmed faith.

Please do not think that you are doing God a favour in believing in him and in condescending to become a Christian. As we thought when we considered repentance, we are requested to lay down the arms of our rebellion without delay, to confess our sinfulness as the tax-gatherer did and to swear our allegiance to him. We should do this not merely because it happens to be in our interest to do so, but because the very dignity and glory and holiness of God demand that we surrender and submit.

And if we hesitate to commit ourselves, are we not casting doubt upon the integrity of God? If we hesitate, are we not implying that God does not really have our best interests at heart? It seems that we are afraid that God may intend to limit us and hedge us about with restrictions to a small, petty, narrow life. He promises to give us an abundant life, to bring us into an apprehension of reality and an appreciation and sensitivity to all that God has created, and a consciousness of the needs of other people, and a fresh realisation of our own destiny and, at long last, a purpose and point to life. Let us realise what we are implying by our hesitation to trust him. We are denying that God is good and that his will is good and acceptable and perfect.

'Brinkmanship' is the art of hesitating while we ask the question, 'Dare we face the consequences?' Some of us are past masters of this. Some of us, however, just dither. 'Do I just jump? Do I stop to look? I know I can do a standing jump but it is quite different on top of a chasm!'

How long, then, will you hesitate on the brink? Sheldon Vanauken, an American converted at Oxford, who corresponded with C. S. Lewis, is most helpful as he talks about the need for this leap of faith.

> Christianity had come to seem to us *probable*. It all hinged on this Jesus. Was he, in fact, the Lord Messiah, the Holy One of Israel, the Christ? Was he, indeed, the incarnate God? Very God of very God? This was the heart of the matter. *Did* he rise from the dead? The apostles, the evangelists, Paul believed it with utter conviction. Could we believe on their belief ... Christianity ... in a word, the divinity of Jesus ... seemed probable to me. But there is a gap between the probable and proved. How was I to cross it? If I were

to stake my whole life on the risen Christ, I wanted proof. I wanted certainty. I wanted to see him eat a bit of fish. I wanted letters of fire across the sky. I got none of these. And I continued to hang about on the edge of the gap . . . The position was not, as I had been comfortably thinking all these months, merely a question of whether I was to accept the Messiah or not. It was a question of whether I was to accept him – or *reject*. My God! There was a gap *behind* me, too. Perhaps the leap to acceptance was a horrifying gamble – but what of the leap to rejection? There might be no certainty that Christ was God – but, by God, there was no certainty that he was not. This was not to be borne. I could not reject Jesus. There was only one thing to do, once I had seen the gap behind me. I turned away from it and flung myself over the gap towards Jesus.

Early on a damp English morning with spring in the air, I wrote in the Journal and to C. S. Lewis: 'I choose to believe in the Father, Son and Holy Ghost – in Christ, my Lord and my God. Christianity has the ring, the feel, of unique truth.'[2]

I find this picture extraordinarily compelling – this picture of a man who not only finds a yawning gulf to faith to be jumped in front of him, but suddenly realises that there is an even bigger jump to be made backwards, and that his position is crumbling. He may only regard it as probable that Jesus is God, but what certainty is there that he was not God?

What are we to do to get off the horns of this dilemma? Paul gives us a helpful description of what is necessary for a person to become a Christian:

If you confess with your mouth, 'Jesus is Lord,' and believe in your heart that God raised him from the dead, you will be saved. For it is with your heart that

you believe and are justified, and it is with your mouth
that you confess and are saved. As the Scripture says,
'Everyone who trusts in him will never be put to
shame.' For there is no difference between Jew and
Gentile – the same Lord is Lord of all and richly
blesses all who call on him, for, 'Everyone who calls on
the name of the Lord will be saved' (Rom. 10: 9–13).

According to these verses above, it is with the *heart* that
we believe and with the *tongue* that we confess, and both
these things are necessary to becoming a Christian. We
believe in our hearts as fact that God has raised him from
the dead, thus vindicating him as his Son, and vindicating
all that he claimed about himself. But then, the step of faith
is necessary to confess him with the mouth. We are to
commit ourselves by confessing publicly that Jesus is Lord.
This is not only a confession of his divinity, but a commitment to his service. I am confessing that he is *my* Lord.
Many people have found that their sense of commitment
was greatly helped by going and telling some sympathetic
Christian that they are now believing in Jesus and, by
confessing with their mouths that this is so, their faith is
strengthened. I hope you will find that.

I remember meeting a Japanese at some large Crusade
meetings in Tokyo. Sometimes, evangelists from overseas
fail to realise that you cannot follow exactly the same
practice in a country which has a different cultural understanding. The Japanese were invited to put their hands up
if they wanted to become Christians and to come up to the
front.

Japanese are exceedingly polite people. One person turned
to me and said, 'Is it all right if I don't go forward?' When
people have gone to such efforts to arrange nice music and a
well-organised meeting and, clearly, the intended conclusion is that people should put up their hands or come and
stand at the front, then who would be so discourteous as to
disappoint them? And if courtesy will not bring people to

the front, then curiosity will, for one wonders just what will happen to people who do go to the front and, indeed, if free booklets are offered as well, even natural cupidity will bring people to the front.

Of course, if you explain to people that, in becoming a Christian, they are giving their life-long allegiance to Jesus as their 'feudal Lord', just as Japanese Samurai did in all their history and drama, and that becoming a Christian means obeying all the commands of Jesus to the letter and serving him to the death, then not many people will come forward. But they will know what you mean.

This particular man put his hand up and went to the front, but told me that he felt no different and returned home very confused. Was he or was he not a Christian? He remembered that Christians read their Bibles, so he tried that. Then he remembered that Christians pray. He had never prayed before and didn't know any suitable words to say, but started in his own words as best as he could and began to speak the words 'Syuu Iesu . . . (Lord Jesus)'. 'And then,' he said, 'the moment that I prayed and called on him, I knew that he was real.' As soon, in other words, as he called upon the name of the Lord, he was saved. It doesn't say whoever puts his hand up or whoever goes to the front, but it does say whoever calls upon the name of the Lord.

May I suggest that you should do just that. You may wish to do it here and now, or you may wish to think about it and then call upon his name. If you are afraid of being moved by the emotional moment, then wait until the cold, unromantic dawn. It would be quite wrong to make a crucial decision like this merely on the basis of emotion, although it is very difficult to take any meaningful step in relationships without some emotion appearing as a by-product, but then there is no reason to be afraid of that. All I would like to say is that when you have committed yourself, you ought then to go and tell some sympathetic Christian that you know and confess with your mouth that

Jesus is Lord. Later you can try telling somebody who
might be unsympathetic.

At the time of his conversion, Vanauken wrote:

> Did Jesus live? And did He really say
> the burning words that banish mortal fear?
> And are they true? Just this is central, here,
> The Church must stand or fall. It's *Christ* we weigh.
>
> All else is off the point: the flood, the day,
> Of Eden, or the Virgin Birth – Have done.
> The question is, did God send us the Son
> Incarnate, crying Love? Love is the way!
>
> Between the probable and proved there yawns
> A gap. Afraid to jump, we stand absurd,
> then see *behind* us sink the ground and, worse,
> our very stand-point crumbling.
> Desperate dawns our only hope:
> To leap into the Word, that opens up the shuttered
> universe.[3]

Chapter 9

THE RETURN OF THE KING

If you saw a company of pilgrims walking as if for a wager, each one with his teeth set, and if you happened to ask them one after another: whither they were going? And from each you were to receive the same answer that positively they were all in such a hurry that they had never found leisure to enquire into the nature of their errand, confess, my dear sir, you would be startled at the indifference they exhibited. Am I going too far if I say that this is the condition of the large majority of our fellow men and almost all our fellow women.

(Robert Louis Stevenson)

There have probably been few more damaging misunderstandings of Christian belief, both as a mistaken view held by non-believers and as a view propagated by some Christians, that the Christian faith is primarily concerned with the next world and posthumous benefits alleged to be available there. Where will you spend eternity? asks the tract. You would rather go to heaven than hell, wouldn't you? . . . Please sign on the dotted line!

All this tends to perpetuate the idea that Christianity is a kind of eternal life-insurance policy or fire escape from hell: which means that you can postpone making any decision until a last-moment death-bed repentance. That was rather easier when death-beds were more lingering affairs, after being thrown from a horse or sickening with an ague. Nowadays, car accidents, strokes and heart attacks leave little opportunity for what the Book of Common Prayer called 'time for amendment of life'. Doubtless, life expectancy is longer than it used to be, but the possibility of a sudden and unexpected death seems to have increased.

From the earlier chapters we should have already understood that being a Christian is not simply a matter of signing an eternal life-insurance policy, getting a ticket to heaven and twiddling your thumbs until you go. We should have seen that to spend a day longer living estranged and alienated from God, hostile and disobedient to him, is an affront to our Creator, the living God, who gives life to all things and gives us all things richly to enjoy. From the Godward side, it is a serious affront to God who longs to bless and to help us, who has spoken to us and is awaiting our response, and who has sent his Son from heaven to die for us on the cross. From the manward side, on our part it is a waste of life to go on living in darkness, when we might walk in the light; to go on selfishly living for ourselves either actively or passively aligned with the enemies of God. He wants us to repent and return, and to be reconciled with him. He wants to restore us by giving us new life. And we are wasting and spoiling our lives, and frustrating our true purpose until we do return to him. He wants us to know joy and gladness, and go leaping and dancing into life.

Those of us who have tried both ways of living know that there is no comparison. Life without hope and without God is so pointless, like a book without a plot and without an end. Life with God is to be in harmony with our Creator and in tune with the universe. It is true that some aspects of the Christian faith are world-denying, and that Christ calls us to crucify our selfish natures every day. But it is also true that when we become Christians, it is world-transfiguring: we enter upon a new consciousness of the wonder and beauty of the created world around us and, because of Christ, to a heightened appreciation of other people and the uniqueness of their personalities.

A CHRISTIAN VIEW OF DEATH

Having said all this, however, we must not underestimate
the significance of the Christian attitude towards death.
Even busy young people, in the exuberant Gadarene rush
into adult life, must reflect on the fact that they have lived a
quarter of their lives already. And where is all this leading?

Surely – to death.

And, surely, it is sensible sometimes to pause and think
about our destination.

It may be the death of a relative or, perhaps, fear of our
own death which drives us sometimes to think very seriously about death. The following poem 'Before the Anaesthe-
tic' or 'A Real Fright' seems to have been written when
lying in the Radcliffe Infirmary listening to the bells of St
Giles:

> The mellow bells are ringing round
> And charge the evening light with sound,
> And I look motionless from bed
> On heavy trees and purple red
> And hear the midland bricks and tiles
> Throw back the bells of stone St Giles,
> Bells, ancient now as castle walls,
> Now hard and new as pitchpine stalls,
> Now full with help from ages past,
> Now dull with death and hell at last.
> Swing up! and give me hope of life,
> Swing down! and plunge the surgeon's knife.
> I, breathing for a moment, see
> Death wing himself away from me
> And think, as on this bed I lie,
> Is it extinction when I die?[1]

There is, then, this fearful attitude towards death but
the Christian comment of Professor C. A. Coulson is an

interesting contrast. 'When you get old like I am (sixty), the last really exciting thing you've got to look forward to is death. You have done almost everything you can do in this world by then.'

It is certainly important that Christians should have real answers.

I stood the other day and watched a man and his four children standing in front of a coffin containing the discarded remains of his wife and their mother. It is not that they had discarded her, but she had discarded her body like a glove which the hand within no longer needed.

A few years ago, I came back to my desk and found a ransom note addressed personally to me by two of our Leprosy Clinic nurses in South Thailand. They had been kidnapped, and a year later their bodies were found shot through the back of the head. A Swiss missionary friend was shot and robbed on the trail, and his body left for the flies and the rats and for his wife to find the next day.

These are all situations of death that I have had to face in recent years.

Even while relatively young, we begin to meet death: our grandparents and then our uncles and aunts, and our parents and then, later, our brothers and sisters, friends, contemporaries, and then people younger than ourselves.

We are glad then not to be able to offer people vague, pious hopes that ring so hollow, but the straightforward teaching of Jesus. He taught us to live this present life with an eye on the next. He told men in general to store up for themselves treasure in heaven, and told one rich young ruler in particular to give all his possessions to the poor, in order that he might have treasure in heaven. He spoke of the rich man who had been careless of the poor man suffering at his gate and now suffering torments in hell.

So, we have to notice that the future, the life to come, and heaven are all still part of the Christian message. They are not the whole message, but they are still a part of the message, and a part which leads purpose to the whole: it would be a bit pointless if there were no end, no destination, no winding up of the present proceedings.

THE RETURN OF THE KING

In Christian thinking, part of the answer to death is the expected return of the King. Christians not only believe that the pre-existent Christ first came into this world to be born as the baby Jesus in Bethlehem, and then to die on the cross and to rise again, but Christians have always believed that Jesus Christ would return to this world not, this time, in weakness as a baby, but rather in force and majesty as a King. Jesus himself taught this, and Christians have always confessed it in the Creed: 'And he will come again in glory to judge the living and the dead, and his kingdom will have no end' (The Nicene Creed).

Some of you may feel that I am spoiling the discussion by introducing all this supernatural stuff – Jesus coming back again and all that. A moment's examination will show the relevance of all this. After all, looked at from a Christian point of view, what else is the first visit, the birth into this world of the pre-existent Son of God, but supernatural? What else, for that matter, is your meeting God now? And what, after all, is Christian belief in prayer, if it does not involve the supernatural? Christianity without the supernatural is like geometry without lines!

The Christian world-view expects an end: lives come to an end, books draw to a conclusion; journeys come to an end; trains reach the terminus; symphonies normally finish; the match is over at the final whistle; students graduate; wars end. It would thus seem rather strange if the world did not come to an end. The view of the Bible is that everything will come to a final dénouement with the return of the King. Life is not like a kind of endless revue, where each performer does his turn and then goes out through the wings to get his wages. It is more like an opera, where the whole cast come forward at the end for the judgment of the watchers, and the bouquets fly through the air on to the stage. Christians, then, expect the return of their King.

It may be objected that something unique, like this, is very difficult to believe. The occurrence of remarkable events is always difficult to imagine beforehand.

The eruption of Vesuvius, the Tokyo earthquake, the Hiroshima and Nagasaki atom bombs, men landing on the moon and the San Francisco earthquake when it takes place. All have something of an unreal quality about them.

I remember as a schoolboy staring fascinated into the sky at the vapour trails and the sound of machine guns at the onset of the Battle of Britain. It all seemed so totally unreal, until the scared voice of my mother awoke me: 'Come back into the house at once, you naughty boy!' But, after five or six years spent at war, the end of the European War was like a happy, unreal dream after the reality of the nightmare years. I can still remember us schoolboys standing round a burning haystack with effigies of Hitler and Mussolini. And then on that unique occasion, so unlike normally reserved schoolboys, holding hands and singing, and feeling that we stood on the edge of a new world.

Surely, the return of the King will have something of that same quality, as well as making all human pageantry of coronations, Olympic Games, royal weddings and jubilees seem relatively minor affairs.

The Bible speaks graphically about the return of the King:

> We believe that Jesus died and rose again and so we believe that God will bring with Jesus those who have fallen asleep in him. According to the Lord's own word, we tell you that we who are still alive, who are left till the coming of the Lord, will certainly not precede those who have fallen asleep. For the Lord himself will come down from heaven, with a loud command, with the voice of the archangel and with the trumpet

call of God, and the dead in Christ will rise first. After
that, we who are still alive and are left will be caught
up with them in the clouds to meet the Lord in the air.
And so we will be with the Lord for ever (1 Thess. 4:
14–17).

The word repeatedly used for 'the coming of the Son of
Man' in the teaching of Jesus or 'his coming' in the teaching
of the apostles, is the word *parousia* which from the time
of the Ptolemies of Egypt onward, had a quasi-technical
meaning of *a royal visit*. The New Testament begins with the
genealogies of kings, the wise men from the East asking
'Where is he that is born King of the Jews?' The ministry of
Jesus begins with his going round the synagogues 'herald-
ing the gospel of the kingdom'. Each one of these words has
a royal sound. The word gospel itself does, for it is not mere
'good news', but good news about a king proclaimed with
authority. The 'Court Circular' in *The Times* could be called
evangelion (good news). The announcement of the birth of a
prince or of any royal action would be such a 'gospel'. It
carries also an authoritative ring, without apology and with
no 'perhaps', but something to be proclaimed and heralded
with the authority of the King of Kings. Words like Lord
and Saviour were both used extensively in emperor worship, rather as Cromwell used to be referred to as Lord
Protector. When we looked at Philippians 2 (in Chapter 2)
we realised that there has already been a coronation of
Jesus Christ, following his ascension, and the New Testament looks forward to a coming royal visit of the King,
when every knee will bow in homage before him. This royal
language of thrones and crowns is found everywhere in the
New Testament.

In I Thessalonians 4 above Paul is dealing with the
problem of death. It seems probable that he had already
taught the Thessalonians about Christ's future 'royal
coming' but meanwhile some Christians had died. Questions
were arising in the minds of the Christians about their

status. Would they miss all the fun? Would their dying mean that they would never see this anticipated great and glorious jubilee to end all jubilees?

Paul tells the Thessalonian Christians that they are not to grieve like 'the rest who have no hope'. The world today is still full of this fatalistic resignation to death on the part of those who have 'no hope'. And yet there is in the human heart a longing that those whom we love might be real – that we might in an after-life again have the opportunity for conscious reunion with those whom we have loved.

This, Paul reminds them, is found in the Christian gospel: 'We believe that Jesus died and rose again and so we believe that God will bring with Jesus those who have fallen asleep in him.' In other words, that when that great 'royal visit' takes place, those who have died believing in Christ will return with him and, so far from missing out on that momentous event, will in fact be a jump ahead, as it were, of those who are still alive and remaining on earth when he comes.

As a missionary I have worked in countries conditioned by Buddhist understanding of this present world as a subjective illusion passing across the television screen of my consciousness. I am experiencing dreams and nightmares which move relentlessly on and in which the major characters whom I have loved are never seen again. What a glorious relief to offer them the robust and concrete Christian expectation of a reunion with those who have fallen asleep in Jesus.

Do you know what a cemetery is? A place to bury the dead, you reply. The word cemetery is derived from the Greek verb used here three times for falling asleep. A cemetery is thus, more correctly, a Christian dormitory! The word itself is used only three times in the New Testament for literal sleep, and on the other fifteen occasions for Christians who have died. Except that Christians are never said to 'die' in the New Testament – they only fall asleep. Most of us are not afraid to fall asleep. By contrast, at the end of a busy day, we feel tired and weary and it's a wonderful relief to get to bed and lie down and drift straight off to sleep. Thus, the good bishop, Thomas Ken, wrote:

> Teach me to live, that I may dread,
> The grave as little as my bed

Jesus is not said to sleep: 'Jesus died'. One of the results of the unique death of Jesus on the cross is that now for us death becomes merely a prolonged sleep as we wait for Christ's royal return. He died that we might sleep.

So, you see that the Christian message does also have something to say about death and Christ's victory over it, removing the fear from it. There will, of course, be grief for those who are left behind and feel a sense of loneliness and sadness at losing the company of those whom they have loved, but it is not fatalistic misery of those without hope, for whom death is the end. We must not be superficial here. Christians will certainly grieve, but not like those who have no hope.

We are not saying in a glib and facile way that Christians have no problems about death, but they are problems of grieving in the loneliness of losing those whom we have loved, rather than fear about one's own death. We are to 'fall asleep' looking forward to that glorious awaking, when we are roused in order to accompany the King on his royal visit. God will bring with the returning Christ those who have fallen asleep in him. Those who are alive and remain will go out to meet the coming King, and the word used here for 'going out to meet' was a technical term used for the reception committee that went out to meet an emperor on the occasion of a royal visit.

There will be no more doubt, when that day comes, about the reality of Christ and the fact of his resurrection. We have seen earlier that the giving of the Holy Spirit to make Christ real to each one of us in our hearts is infinitely preferable to a risen Christ as the object of pilgrimage to Jerusalem, but, ultimately, there will be the overwhelming awe and wonder of experiencing the reality of the Christian message.

'The Lord himself' will descend from heaven. The words used emphasise both the suddenness and the majesty by using vivid apocalyptic imagery. As the heads of soldiers snap back with the shouted word of command, and as the heralds' trumpets blast out the great fanfare that makes our blood run faster, so Christ will be shown to all people as Lord and King, and every knee will bow to him.

FOR THE PRESENT . . .

We have seen, then, that the future royal coming of Christ is very relevant to the whole matter of death. However, Jesus himself was concerned to remind us that it is also relevant to the whole matter of life, and how we spend it. It is not only that the return of Christ is significant because it will mean the resurrection of those who died believing in Jesus, but it will also be significant as calling to account those who are still alive. The Christian message is not just relevant to us when we die, because Christ is coming back as King, but also extremely relevant to how we spend the time until the King comes back.

In Luke's gospel, there are accounts of nine or ten different dinner parties, banquets and evening meals. Jesus himself seems to have been extremely popular as an after-dinner speaker, when he told a number of memorable stories. We mentioned earlier that, after the senior tax collector in Jericho, a little short man called Zacchaeus, had been converted, he threw a 'repentance party' for all his friends, so that he could announce his new allegiance to Jesus and also so that they could meet Jesus for themselves. And after they had eaten, Jesus told a story about the servants of a

man who was going to come back again as king. When he
went away he gave each of his servants a sum of money and
told them, 'Put this money to work until I come back.'
On his return, each one was called to give an account
of his transactions. Most had invested the money wisely
and could report profits, but one said, 'Sir, here is your
mina; I have kept it laid away in a piece of cloth. I was
afraid of you, because you are a hard man. You take out
what you did not put in and reap what you did not sow.'
The obvious reply to this pathetic excuse was, 'Well if you
knew all this, why didn't you do something about it!' And
so the wise king gave this carefully preserved sum to the
servant who had already shown most business acumen. He
summed up his policy in the words, 'To everyone who has,
more will be given, but as for the one who has nothing,
even what he has will be taken away.' And the Bible tells
us that this parable was told for those who 'thought that
the kingdom of God was going to appear at once' (Luke 19:
11–26).

All the servants received the same initial amount of
capital to work with.[2] Every one of us has one life to use.
We all have the same number of hours in a day and of
days in a year. The society in which Christians are called
to live is one which is hostile to them and to their King.
They are, as it were, a subversive movement of royalists
working for the return of the King to a people who have
declared a republic and thus, in a hostile society, they have
to go out and risk their capital in a competitive market.
Will they merely seek to preserve what they have selfishly
for themselves and give it back to the King when he returns,
or are they prepared to trade and work for him and to risk
their all in the market, for his sake? As Christians we are
called to face this element of danger and risk in a world
which is largely hostile or indifferent to the claims of Jesus
as King.

Tom Howard, realising that he is in touch 'not with the
pale Galilean, but with the towering and furious figure

who will not be managed', goes on to say 'we found Him towering above us, scorching our efforts into clinkers, and recalling us to wildness and *risk* and humility and love'.[3] If you become a Christian as a result of reading this book, I hope that you will not be one of the wishy-washy, uncommitted kind, but one who will respond to Christ's call 'to wildness and risk and humility and love'.

The Christian faith, then, is not merely a matter of ensuring that one is a servant of the King; but of actually serving him. The Christian is not somebody who is content to have saved his own skin and assured his own destiny by becoming a Christian, a servant of Christ in name. I was thrilled on the Monday after a mission, when somebody who had only decided to be a Christian about three days earlier said, 'I have suddenly realised that I became a Christian for the wrong reasons.' Not everybody comes to that realisation so quickly. The incredible humility and mercy of God is shown in his readiness to accept us when we return to him in the first place for predominantly personal and selfish reasons. We want our sins forgiven, we want our vices removed and virtues added, we want an end to alienation and estrangement, we want to be better people.

And we want it for ourselves.

One of the first things that the servant has to realise is that his being a Christian is not so much that he may be saved, but that he may serve. The real motive for becoming a Christian is that it's quite wrong to be anything else, and an affront to the holiness and majesty of our King. Because he is the kind of person that he is, who can but serve him? But, for the most part, we come for far less altruistic reasons, and we need to see at once that being a Christian is not so much a state that we have achieved as a service which we have entered. We must *work* for the kingdom.

What sort of person is the man who brought back his original capital unused? He was a man who wasted his opportunities. You all have one life to use or waste. We all have equally the one life to use to serve the King. What are you going to do with yours?

You may bury it in some suburb, wrapped up in a handkerchief of comfortable affluence. In other words, you can do nothing with your capital, you can fritter it away, secure only in being a Christian, but really leading as pointless and useless a life as if you had not become a Christian at all. The man in the parable was a *status quo* man, satisfied with things as they are. He would be perfectly content with going to church and having a church to go to. He did not see that the church is meant to be the caterpillar stage of the new society, and he was not working to build God's kingdom.

One cannot escape the impression that many so-called Christians potter along quite happily, preserving their own faith in healthy condition and going along to churches, chapels and other Christian groups for a spiritual top-up when necessary. Are we really working for our King in the place where he has put us? Will you too catch fire and start working for our King now? We really are a kind of 'underground movement' working quietly and steadily for the return of the rightful King. Will you go through life clutching your 'capital', unused, untraded with, and looking for a nice, quiet suburb somewhere with nice, quiet neighbours and a nice quiet school for your nice, quiet children? Will you bury your eternal capital in the barren lands of affluence? Or will you have already built up to three or four pounds of capital when you have finished studying, and will the whole of your life be fruitful and productive for his kingdom? Are you going to live that life just for yourself, content just in being a Christian, or will you be a loyal, faithful, hardworking servant ready to go and live in the inner city, to labour in some down-town Samaria, in order to work for your coming King? Would you be willing, indeed, and ready to go to the ends of the earth to trade for him, however dangerous the roads and the markets?

But, perhaps you are not yet committed? Let me conclude

the book by explaining very briefly, using the figure of a King and the kingdom that we have been using in this chapter, what steps are necessary to become a Christian.

1. We must admit our rebellion

We have been refusing to accept God's sovereignty and have been living in a state of defiant hostility, either pretending that God does not exist, or in a state of treasonable opposition to him. This state of alienation is a miserable one and we must confess that we have sinned against him.

2. God has declared an amnesty

Christ has died and risen again and will be returning in judgment. If we will lay down now the arms of our rebellion, he offers us a free pardon (forgiveness of sins) and reinstatement as servants, with full rights and privileges (reconciliation) and, still more, he goes on to offer to us (did you ever hear of such clemency!) the status of royal princes, sons and daughters of the household ('adopted as his sons', Eph. 1: 5). There never were such merciful and generous terms offered to rebels as these. How could we ever be so foolish as to refuse?

3. We surrender to him

We accept his terms and bow our knees in surrender, confessing our rebellion, asking forgiveness and accepting pardon. We will find that he will soon raise us up from our knees to receive his royal welcome.

C. S. Lewis describes it beautifully:

> The voices spoke again; but not loud this time. They were awed and trembled. 'He is coming' they said. 'The God is coming into his house . . .'
>
> The air was growing brighter and brighter about us; as if something had set it on fire. Each breath I drew let into me new terror, joy, overpowering sweetness. I was pierced through and through with the arrows of it. I

was being unmade. I was no-one . . . The earth and stars and sun, all that was or will be, existed for his sake. And he was coming. The most dreadful, the most beautiful, the only dread and beauty there is, was coming. The pillars on the far side of the pool flushed with his approach. I cast down my eyes.[4]

APPENDIX

DOWN TO EARTH QUESTIONS COMMONLY ASKED
BY DOWN TO EARTH PEOPLE

While the argument forms part of a whole chapter or section of the book, it may be helpful to pinpoint certain common objections as they occur in the text, where at least partial answers may be found. Those listed here may be referred to at more than one point in the text, and there is inevitably some overlap with similar questions in this index.

NOTES

CHAPTER 1

1. The idea that miracles were invented to impress falls down again because, interestingly, John the Baptist who also had a very large following almost at the same time as Jesus, is not credited with any miracles at all (John 10: 41), even though it was John the Baptist who himself bore witness to Jesus and identified him as the Messiah.

2. It is not always realised that there are secular references establishing the historicity of Jesus Christ. 'The name Christian comes to them from Christ, who was executed in the reign of Tiberius by the procurator Pontius Pilate' (AD 112, Tacitus, Governor of Asia, in *Annals*, 1544).

There is an inscription discovered at Nazareth in which Claudius (Emperor AD 41–54) expresses his displeasure at reports of the removal of dead bodies from tombs, giving warning that any further tampering with graves will incur the death penalty.

Suetonius records that Claudius expelled the Jews from Rome because they were constantly making disturbances at the instigation of one 'Chrestos' (AD 49, Life of Claudius, 25.4).

While many have suspected a later interpolation, though there is no actual manuscript evidence for this, because it is thought improbable that a Jew would acknowledge Jesus as Messiah, the references to Jesus as a historical character are significant:

'And there arose about this time (the time of Pilate, AD 26–36) Jesus, a wise man, if indeed we should call him a man; for he was a doer of marvellous deeds, a teacher of men who received the truth with pleasure. He won over many Jews and also many Greeks. This man was the Messiah. And when Pilate had condemned him to the cross at the instigation of our own leaders, those who had s8o1c1

loved him from the first did not cease for he appeared to them on the third day alive again, as the holy prophets had predicted and said many wonderful things about him. And even now the race of Christians, so named after him, have not died out.' (Josephus, *Antiquities of the Jews*, 18.3.3).

3. It is better to use a model whereby God holds all things in existence like images on a TV screen. For a development of this idea, see Prof. Donald Mackay, *The Clockwork Image*, (IVP, 1974), p. 59.

4. Tom Howard, *Christ the Tiger* (Hodder & Stoughton, 1967), p. 9.

CHAPTER 2

1. My wife and I lived and worked in Japan as missionaries for ten years, and indeed have continued to work with Japanese people ever since.

2. In Japan when a crown prince succeeds his father as emperor he is given a new dynastic name. Each emperor has a special name which attaches to the new era, and provides a traditional way of dating. The Name given to the crowned and enthroned Son is not 'Jesus', the Greek form of the Hebrew name 'Joshua' for that was given to him at his birth as a human baby. It was a relatively common name given to Jewish babies at that time, being probably the first name of the criminal Barabbas, and certainly of Paul's fellow worker 'Jesus, who is called Justus' (Col. 4: 11).

3. We should also notice that this name of Lord is shared by the Holy Spirit (2 Cor. 3: 17–18). See Chapter 5.

The Shema, the daily recitation by Orthodox Jews reads, 'Hear, O Israel: The Lord our God, the Lord is One. Love the Lord your God with all your heart and with all your soul and with all your strength' (Deut. 6: 4–5) and with equal clarity, the New Testament declares, 'There is one God and one mediator between God and men, the man Christ Jesus' (1 Tim. 2: 5), who now shares in the personal name of the Father. However, we should be clear that Christians, like Jews and Muslims, only believe in One God and not in three. We believe in three Persons in One Godhead, who share one name.

CHAPTER 4

1. Tom Howard, *ibid.*, p. 126.

CHAPTER 5

1. F. W Neitzsche, *Thus Spake Zarathustra* (Penguin, 1969), p. 68.

2. From the song 'Nobody Dances' by Aime Duval, in *Faith, Folk and Festivity* (Galliard, 1969).

3. All of this is worked out in most tremendous and careful detail in the Bampton Lectures, preached before the University of Oxford in 1866 by Canon Professor H. T. Liddon, entitled 'The Divinity of Christ'.

Arguments about theism rather than atheism or agnosticism never seem to get very far – perhaps because they are so theoretical. But that can all be short-circuited by asking about the person of Jesus of Nazareth, as indeed many of his contemporaries did: Who is this man? What kind of man is he? And this is the central question upon which the truth of Christianity stands or falls. Was he no more than a remarkably good man, or was he who he claimed to be: God taking human form and coming 'down to earth' on our behalf?

For further reading try *Basic Christianity*, J. R. W. Stott (IVP).

4. This drama was performed by Anne Atkins at the Oxford Mission mentioned in the foreword.

CHAPTER 6

1. Dorothy L. Sayers, *The Mind of the Maker*, Methuen, 1947, Chapter 3.

2. Joseph Bayly, *Psalms of My Life* (Tyndale House, 1969), p. 48, 'A psalm of personal need'.

CHAPTER 7

1. Phil Thomson.

CHAPTER 8

1. Coleridge expressed this in a clear but complicated fashion when he wrote: 'It could not be intellectually more evident without becoming morally less effective; without counteracting its own end

by sacrificing the life of faith to the cold mechanism of a worth-less, because compulsory, assent' *Biographia Literaria* (Everyman), p. 106.

2. *A Severe Mercy*, pp. 94, 98, 99.

3. Sheldon Vanauken, *A Severe Mercy* (Hodder & Stoughton, 1979) p. 100.

CHAPTER 9

1. John Betjeman.

2. This story differs from the rather similar story told by the Lord Jesus on a different occasion (Matt. 25: 14–30), when the servants were each given different amounts of capital, depending on their gifts and abilities.

3. Tom Howard, *Christ the Tiger* (Hodder & Stoughton, 1967), pp. 9, 124.

4. C. S. Lewis, *Till We Have Faces* (Collins, 1956), pp. 306–7.